Knife  for Martial Artists

by Martina Sprague

Copyright 2015 Martina Sprague

No part of this book may be reproduced in any form or by any means, electronic or otherwise, without the prior written consent of the author. All books contained in this volume are copyright by Martina Sprague.

Disclaimer: Always use caution and never use real knives when practicing the martial arts exercises in this book. The reader assumes full responsibility for injuries incurred by doing the exercises described herein, and for the use or misuse of any information contained in this book. The author does not endorse the use of edged weapons as a means for resolving conflict. The instruction in this book is purely informational in purpose and intended to strengthen the martial artist's empty-hand skills.

Acknowledgements: Front cover image source: Martina Sprague. Back cover image pictures modern karambit. Image source: Martina Sprague. Image source for horse logo (slightly adapted) on back cover: CoralieM Photographie, reproduced under Wikimedia Commons license.

PREFACE TO THE KNIFE DEFENSE VOLUME

The *Knife Training Methods and Techniques for Martial Artists* series gives the martial arts interested person a solid background on the importance of the knife as a combat weapon, inspires the reader about the benefits of knife training, and provides detailed instruction in how to manipulate and defend against a knife with speed, proficiency, and confidence.

Almost any martial art, traditional or modern, can be adapted to knife offense and defense without changing the basic principles of the art. Since the knife is a relatively small and lightweight weapon, many of the moves and movement patterns you use in your empty-hand art are easily transferable to your knife techniques, and vice versa. The practical lessons you learn by adding knife training to your arsenal include quick reaction skills, physical and mental control, footwork and evasion tactics, distance control, and target precision. Knife training gives you a decided physical and mental edge and opens new dimensions that will deepen your understanding of the martial arts.

This special volume contains books 6 through 10 of the *Knife Training Methods and Techniques for Martial Artists* series, with focus on defending and counterattacking with the knife (each book can also be purchased separately):

6. Knife Defense Basics

7. Knife Defense Dynamics

8. Knife-on-Knife and Multiple Opponent Knife Defense Strategies

9. Knife and Empty-Hand Defenses Compared

10. Knife Training and Advanced Martial Arts Concepts

Knife Defense Basics, book 6 in the series, covers basic knife defense principles, how to recognize a threat and prepare a defense, the importance of seizing the initiative and counterstriking, superior positioning along with an analysis of safety in distance versus closeness, and a number of blocking, deflection, and countering exercises. It ends with a discussion of different types of threats and how to choose a training method that is right for you.

Knife Defense Dynamics, book 7 in the series, covers dynamic knife defense concepts including seizing the initiative, forcing the adversary to retreat, and taking his balance. It covers different ways to defend against and neutralize the threat in stand-up and ground scenarios. It also includes a discussion about the knife as a weapon of coercion.

Knife-on-Knife and Multiple Opponent Knife Defense Strategies, book 8 in the series, covers commonly taught knife strategies and the factors one must be cautious of when fighting multiple opponents. It discusses knife techniques against single opponents armed with a knife, with emphasis on the training benefits yet dangers of dueling with the knife. It ends with more than a dozen martial arts dummy and partner exercises for further practice and analysis.

Knife and Empty-Hand Defenses Compared, book 9 in the series, demonstrates how most empty-hand and knife techniques are interchangeable, or nearly so, with only minor adjustments. The knife can thus be used as an enhancement tool to build speed and precision in your empty-hand techniques. Moreover, should you find yourself in a self-defense situation where you have access to a knife, the muscle memory you have developed by practicing the techniques in your empty-hand martial art will be easily transferable to a large arsenal of knife techniques.

Knife Training and Advanced Martial Arts Concepts, book 10 in the series, covers the importance of moving from the mechanical to the conceptual stage of learning successful defenses against knife attacks, the relationship between time and timing, factors that trigger the natural speed of your body, how distance and movement can prove elusive, and different ways to disarm the opponent of the use of his weapons.

Books 1 through 5 of the *Knife Training Methods and Techniques for Martial Artists* series can be found in the *Knife Offense (Five Books in One)* volume, and can also be purchased separately.

Knife Defense Basics

Book 6

Knife Training Methods and Techniques for Martial Artists

by Martina Sprague

TABLE OF CONTENTS

Introduction	9
Brief History	12
Lesson Objectives	15
Thoughts on Basic Knife Defense Principles	16
Pre- and Post-Conflict Stage	22
Superior Positioning and Seizing the Initiative	25
Blocking and Deflecting an Attack	29
Is Safety in Distance or Closeness?	34
Basic Knife Defense Exercises	39
Exercise in Futility or Good Self-Defense Skills?	45
Concluding Thoughts	49

INTRODUCTION

Books 1 through 5 of the *Knife Training Methods and Techniques for Martial Artists* series focused on getting to know and use the knife. Now that you have gained some understanding of knife offense, let's continue by studying what you might do if faced empty handed with a knife-wielding assailant.

If you have experience in a contact martial art, you know that one good strike or kick, even though it may be painful, is not likely to kill you or even end the fight. This bit of knowledge gives you confidence in your survival ability. Participating in contact martial arts training, wearing gloves and other protective gear, is good physical conditioning. It also builds confidence in your ability to take strikes and kicks. But let's assume now that your opponent is armed with a knife, and that a faulty move on your part will likely mean severe injury or death. Will you be more cautious about the techniques you execute, the distance you keep between you and your adversary, or your timing? Even though nothing else has changed, you will approach the situation more cautiously when you know that your safety or life is at stake. Training in knife defense, using a dull training blade and acknowledging each time it touches you, will make you more aware of the dangers involved.

Defending empty handed against the knife is one of the most difficult and dangerous situations you will encounter. When setting up realistic scenarios and training at realistic speed, you will learn that it's not as simple as sidestepping and intercepting the attack, or placing your opponent in a joint lock that neutralizes the threat. You will likely miss the attacker's hand when trying to intercept it and get cut in the process. When facing a knife-wielding attacker, even a cut to a non-lethal area such as your arm can cause shock. If you fail to react with offense after your defensive move, the fight will likely end to your opponent's advantage. When facing a knife-wielding attacker, you must have a keen sense of distance. The fighting range that applies when sparring empty handed in the training hall will likely not be workable against the knife. You must either be far away or very close. If outside of the knife's effective range, you must either distance yourself permanently or find an opportunity to move to close range. You must then control your opponent's offensive capabilities by unbalancing him, harming him through a strike or kick to a vulnerable area, or pinning or controlling his knife-wielding hand.

What are your choices? You can attempt to control the knife, control the arm that holds the knife, or control the person. Untrained people have a tendency to fixate on the knife. But since the knife is at the extension of the arm, it is capable of tremendous speed and is difficult to intercept and control. Focusing on the arm rather than the knife gives you a slightly better chance of achieving control of the weapon without getting cut. Consider, too, the possibility of controlling your opponent's whole body while ignoring the knife initially, through an unbalancing move for instance. Balance loss and damage to your opponent's arms or body may prevent him from gripping or using the knife against you.

As explained in Book 1, the *Knife Training Methods and Techniques for Martial Artists* series has three objectives: The first few books focus on getting to know the knife, its strengths and weaknesses, and on manipulating and using it. The next few books focus on defending against knife attacks. The last few books focus on implementing empty-hand martial arts skills into your knife training, and include scenario-based exercises intended to bring your knowledge into perspective and give you a solid understanding of your strengths and weaknesses when faced with a knife-wielding assailant. Each book starts with an introduction. You are then given the lesson objectives, along with detailed information and a number of training exercises aimed at making you physically and emotionally ready to participate in traditional martial arts demonstrations involving a knife or, if fate will have it, in a real encounter. Remember that it is your responsibility to know and comply with all federal and local laws regarding the possession and carry of edged weapons.

BRIEF HISTORY

Although some people will argue that the techniques you learn in the martial arts training hall are much too complicated for a real situation involving a knife, this is not necessarily true. Remember that many Asian martial arts are built upon surprise tactics. They were developed to give you an advantage over a bigger or stronger adversary. Consider how ancient Chinese military strategist Sun-tzu, for example, advocated surprise and "dirty" fighting; for example, that you should appear weak when you are strong, and strong when you are weak. There is nothing that says that you must use a clean block or clean intercept technique when defending against a knife. Rather, you should find a way to weaken your adversary before engaging him for a disarming technique. Weakening him can involve a distraction such as spitting at his face, or it can involve a strike to a sensitive area such as the eyes.

Moreover, even if you do get cut trying to defend against a knife, it does not necessarily mean that you are completely incapacitated or dead; you may still be able to strike with your bare fists to a vulnerable target and proceed with a disarming technique. Remember that your opponent, too, even though he has a weapon, will experience adrenaline and loss of fine motor skills. An attack that seems precise in a controlled environment will lose that precision on the street. Nobody has a death wish. Your adversary fully knows that if you get hold of the weapon, the odds will likely turn in your favor and against him.

Historical Gem: Not all cuts or thrusts with a sharp weapon prove deadly or even limiting to the victim. Consider, for example, the rapier, which proved a popular dueling weapon in the middle ages. As noted by George Silver, an English gentleman of the sixteenth to seventeenth century known for his writings on swordplay, in his *Paradoxes of Defence* (London, UK: Printed for Edward Blount, 1599), the rapier, due to its extraordinary length, was an article of dress and social function. He did not consider it a true battlefield weapon, however: Although the "science" of dueling and sword fighting for social purposes was "noble" and "preferred next to divinity," which "preserves the soul from hell and the devil," the "noble science" of swordsmanship "defend[s] the body from wounds and slaughter." While the sword, according to Silver, proved lethal and was wielded on the battlefield in the service of a Prince, the rapier, on account of its design as a thrusting rather than slashing weapon, was predictable in motion. Since it was suited only for the thrust, it proved nearly useless in battle. While the rapier could stab deeply into soft tissue, it could not sever a limb or head from the opponent's body. A wounded duelist could thus continue fighting, even after receiving numerous stabs:

> I have known a gentleman hurt in a rapier fight, in nine or ten places throughout the body, arms, and legs, and yet has continued in his fight, and afterward has slain the other, and come home and has been cured of all his wounds without maim, and is yet living.

Every great general in history knows that the moment the first shots are fired, all your plans go out the window. This is true for the knife-wielding attacker as well. Yes, he has the advantage initially, holding both the weapon and the initiative. However, the moment he attacks, and you respond or preempt the attack, the initial plan will likely begin to fail. In fact, he may not even survive the encounter. If his first attempt to stab you fails, he may not have enough endurance to try again with any prospect of success.

An 1874 fencing duel between two gentlemen desiring to settle a dispute the "honorable" way. These sorts of duels resulted in injury more often than death. Image source: Das Wissen des 20. Jahrhunderts, Verlag für Wissenschaft und Bildung, 1961, reproduced under Wikimedia Commons license.

LESSON OBJECTIVES

Upon completion of this lesson, you should:

1. Have acquired a healthy respect for the power of the knife

2. Have gained an understanding of how to retain realism while avoiding injury when training in knife defense techniques with your martial arts buddies

3. Have developed a basic understanding of how issues of violence develop and be able to detect the warning signals

4. Have started to hone your ability to move to a superior position in relation to your opponent, and should understand the importance of seizing the initiative

5. Have had an opportunity to engage in plenty of partner practice involving basic blocks and deflective moves

6. Have gained some knowledge and practical experience in the benefits and pitfalls of distancing yourself from the knife versus moving to close range

7. Have developed insight into the extent to which your empty-hand martial arts background can be used as a guide to building proficiency in basic knife defense

THOUGHTS ON BASIC KNIFE DEFENSE PRINCIPLES

I have heard both extremes: The first position says that when you're attacked by a knife-wielding opponent, you just have to use your *ki*, or internal energy, to snap the knife from the offender's wrist and subdue him by using his own momentum and energy against him. This advice assumes that you have no fear of dying by the knife, and that your opponent will attack with such obviousness that you can easily catch the knife, disarm him, and blend with the momentum of the attack to throw him off balance. The other position says that you'll never pull off a defensive technique against an opponent armed with a knife, because the attack will be like a wild blur and happen faster than any person can possibly time. My view is that neither of these extremes is true. Although it is not easy to defend against a knife-wielding attacker, and you may get injured in the process, it is possible.

Studying the knife and experimenting with a variety of attacks and defenses will give you clarity and insight into what it takes to defend yourself; it will inform you about targets you can strike successfully when under a great deal of stress to protect your life. If a highly skilled person with a knife attacks a lesser skilled student, it is unlikely that the student will pull off an effective defense. When training with the self-proclaimed knife experts in the martial arts training hall, you may encounter those who are eager to explain or show you why your defense won't work, and who profess to know how to counter any defensive technique you suggest. But ask yourself this: Whose game are you playing? Your opponent does not necessarily know your skill or what you are capable of doing. If he did, or if he thought you could hurt him severely and even take the knife from him, he might have second thoughts about attacking you.

A common belief is that a person armed with a knife is less dangerous than a person armed with a firearm. But as noted in the introduction to Book 1 of the *Knife Training Methods and Techniques for Martial Artists* series, edged weapon attacks often end with severe injury to at least one of the combatants. This fact is seldom capitalized on when practicing knife defense and disarming techniques in the martial arts training hall. When studying basic empty-hand defenses against knife attacks, start by exploring a number of factors:

1. How long does it take you to recognize the fact that there is a threat to your life and that the assailant is wielding a knife?

2. How long does it take you to initiate an action intended to avoid the attack?

3. How much distance is between you and the attacker? If your opponent is closer than five feet when you recognize the threat and he or she is intent on using the knife, it may prove difficult to defend against the attack successfully; that is, unless you have received some warning of the attack and are mentally and physically prepared to act immediately.

Any attack with a weapon can potentially have a worse outcome than an unarmed attack. The person with access to the weapon therefore holds the dominant position. If both you and your opponent are armed, it may come down to the "superior" weapon. For example, a gun is superior to a knife from long range. From short range, this is not necessarily true. If you both carry knives, the person with the "superior" knife (generally the longer blade) may hold the dominant position. Although the person with superior skill and willingness to use the knife may dominate the situation, in general a bigger or longer knife is superior to smaller or shorter knife. A big knife has greater capacity to intimidate and greater reach. If you get to the point of physical contact, a bigger knife has the capacity to inflict a deeper and more severe wound.

A firearm is not necessarily limited to a handgun. A rifle or assault weapon could prove impractical for the purpose for which it is intended at grappling range, but might still be used as a tactical weapon to thwart a knife attack, much like you would use a stick or any other object that gives you striking power or leverage. Note that the fighter on the bottom is also controlling the opponent's movement through normal grappling/martial arts techniques by locking his legs around his adversary. Image source: United States Marine Corps, reproduced under Wikimedia Commons license.

However, the dominant position may also belong to the person with superior fighting skills. Superior fighting skills, in turn, depend on a number of factors such as the length and type of your training, your athletic capacity including your physical strength and endurance, and your mental readiness including your willingness to engage the adversary.

If your opponent is brandishing a knife, assume that he is committed to using it. You only have one chance to avoid the first cut. Getting him to commit when it best suits you will likely make your defensive technique stronger.

When exploring the possibilities of prevailing empty handed against an edged weapon, enter the confrontation with the mindset that the fight should last the shortest amount of time possible. You might know the person who threatens you. He or she might be a family member, an acquaintance, or someone you have merely observed repeatedly at a social event. If this is the case, you may also know something about this person's background and training. If not, you will not know how committed he or she is to the attack, or how he will react once you make a move. To increase your chances of success:

1. Have respect for the power of the knife and make an all-out effort to escape injury or death. Avoid the situation completely, if you can.

2. If possible, surprise your opponent and take a cheap shot, such as a strike to the eyes or a kick to the knee. You may even try spitting at his face. If you can't distance yourself, move in with strong offense to end the fight while he is still stunned from your surprise move.

3. In the training hall, allow yourself to experience what it feels like to have your knife hand pinned and your knife taken from you. Knowing what it feels like to have dominance through ownership of a knife, and having that dominance taken from you in the wink of an eye, will give you an indication of how your knife-wielding opponent will feel in a similar situation.

Although you should not assume that you have time to determine whether or not your opponent has a knife or how he intends to use it before you find yourself in the fray, you may also get some forewarning of the dangers that lie ahead. You may have angered your would-be assailant enough to make him reach for the weapon, even if he did not have the intention to use it initially. Consider the brawls that frequently break out at ball games and hockey matches. Those involved may not have had the intent to participate in a fight when they first entered the sports arena.

In the home, domestic violence issues may have been building for some time. The trick is in recognizing these situations long before they develop into knife encounters. Take a moment and think about where the knives are located in your home. The kitchen is an obvious location. You might have a utility knife in the shop in your basement, in your garage, in your closet, or in a drawer. Would it be a good idea to place knives at some other locations in your home? Why or why not?

The greater question may be how you know when it is necessary to use your self-defense skills against a knife-wielding opponent. If you're in an environment conducive to fighting, such as a bar, being observant might inform you of when a fight is beginning to brew. Other indicators of danger include a stranger suddenly grabbing you, unusual noise such as a person screaming, or hurried running as if somebody is trying to get away. But don't assume that these situations necessarily warrant a defensive move. A stranger may simply be patting you on the shoulder in an attempt to get your attention.

PRE- AND POST-CONFLICT STAGE

Now that you have thought about possible knife encounters, it is a good idea to explore the pre- and post-conflict stage. Even if it appears as though an attack comes out of nowhere, there is normally a series of events that lead to the actual attack. When you role play in the training hall, using loud and abusive language, for example, will increase the stress level and bring some realism to the training. Start by identifying several ways in which a conflict might develop. When do you first become aware that you are in danger, or that the situation might escalate? By learning to analyze the situation as rapidly as possible, you will be better prepared to take one of several actions: attempt to flee, preempt the attack, counterattack, or submit to the attacker's demands. Why would you want to submit to the attacker's demands? You don't, really, but making it appear so initially may buy you time to pursue other options. Every person who brandishes a knife does not do so with intent to kill. The knife may also be used as a weapon of coercion.

Your defense comprises three stages. Start by evaluating the situation. Look at how your opponent is holding the knife and determine if it looks like a thrusting or slashing attack. Next, dictate the situation. If you are well-versed in the martial arts and can induce the attack, it might help you seize the initiative. Lastly, eliminate the threat. You do this by relying on previously learned martial arts moves, be it a strike, kick, joint control hold, or balance manipulation. When setting up scenarios in the training hall, ask the following questions:

1. Are you in immediate or imminent danger? How much time is available for developing a response?

2. What type of knife is the attacker using? Different knives have different strengths and weaknesses. How the opponent is holding the knife might indicate the type of attack he or she will use.

3. What is the attacker's motive? Does he want your wallet? Does he want revenge? Does he want to kill you? Why? Might there be an option to deescalate the situation and talk your way out of the encounter?

4. How great is the distance between yourself and the attacker? If the distance is great, ten feet or more, you may find an opportunity to flee. If not, you must either submit initially (or talk your way out of the encounter) or fight. How do you determine when to make your first move?

A weapon gives you power. It can therefore serve as an equalizer against a bigger and stronger opponent. But when facing an armed attacker empty handed, no matter what your size or strength, you must move off the attack line and preferably to a superior position toward your opponent's back. If he or she is wielding a knife, a greater distance is preferred initially. But you must also keep in mind that the average person can cover a distance of twenty feet in as little as a second or two. If you can avoid it, don't go empty handed against a knife-wielding assailant even if you are a highly skilled martial artist. If possible, find something in the vicinity that you can use as a weapon or shield against a stab or cut.

If you know beforehand that you will enter a potentially dangerous situation, it is a good idea to wear some sort of protective clothing; for example, a leather jacket that is difficult to cut through with a knife, or some form of leather protection for your forearms that allows you to use them for blocking an attack without suffering damage to ligaments. Leather gloves, as long as they don't limit the dexterity of your hands, can protect you both when using your fist to strike and when attempting to disarm an adversary. Also think about what type of clothing your opponent is wearing, and counterattack to targets that are unprotected, if possible.

Finally, explore the post-conflict stage. How much damage do you think you and your opponent will suffer in a knife fight, and how do you deal with it?

SUPERIOR POSITIONING AND SEIZING THE INITIATIVE

The bigger person, he or she of greater strength or with a weapon, is generally not he who will benefit the most from self-defense training. To derive the greatest benefit from your studies, you must at least experiment with fighting from the inferior position against a bigger or stronger person (such as on the ground on your back or pinned against a wall with no escape routes available), or you must go empty handed against a weapon. To put the psychological effects of the knife in perspective, if you knew that your opponent had a knife, would you be as eager to close with him, regardless of how much bigger, stronger, or better you are?

If you lose the superior position, it becomes nearly impossible to defend successfully against an opponent armed with a knife and intent on hurting you. Image source: Martina Sprague.

Since the martial arts were typically developed for the benefit of the underdog, attaining the superior position is important in any martial arts endeavor, whether it be karate, kickboxing, grappling, or weapons training. But superior positioning may be particularly important when facing an opponent with a knife or other weapon, because the weapon itself affords him or her superiority.

The superior position is generally away from your opponent's centerline and toward his back, because this position limits the use of his hands. To regain the superior position, he must change the angle at which he is facing you. Maintaining distance from the blade is crucial until you can seize the initiative and move in with your attack. You can also reach superiority through a range of other positions depending on the situation. In a grappling match, for example, the superior position may be the mount (straddling your opponent), or even on your back with your opponent in your guard (between your legs).

When your opponent attacks, be aware of the direction of the blow. Your first concern is to avoid getting cut. You must therefore distance yourself from the reach of the knife, preferably by simultaneously blocking or deflecting the attack. Blocking or deflecting the attack gives you some control and allows you to seize the initiative. Since a knife is most dangerous when in motion, ideally you want to interfere with the free movement of the knife. For example, if your opponent stabs at your midsection, push your hips to the rear while simultaneously blocking the attacking arm. When you have avoided or blocked the attack, immediately proceed with a counterstrike to neutralize the threat.

If unable to distance yourself from the attack, an option is to advance the moment you sense a threat. If you are facing a skilled opponent, however, you may not see much movement prior to the attack. You may now try to take advantage of a lapse in your opponent's concentration, for example, by distracting him with something you say or do. But prepare to execute a defensive move simultaneous with your advance. When stepping forward, be particularly keen on protecting your vital areas, such as your neck. Keep your head shielded behind your shoulder and forearms. If you have to take a cut to your wrists, it is safer taking the cut to the outside rather than inside wrist which holds a lot of blood vessels close to the surface of the skin. What other parts of your body can best withstand cuts, and how can you use these parts to protect your vital areas? I'm not saying that it is okay to get cut, but rather that if you must get cut and you want to live, some parts of your body deserve greater protection than others.

As emphasized in Book 2 of the *Knife Training Methods and Techniques for Martial Artists* series, when facing a knife-wielding opponent the danger is his hands, because this is where the knife is. Even if you can't see a knife in his hand, it may still be present in the reverse grip. You must therefore know where his hands are and what they are doing at all times. Moreover, the knife gives your opponent psychological power that helps him dictate the fight. It is unlikely that he will resort to kicks, for example, when he has a knife available. He or she is also likely to focus the attack on a target above the waist. If you have access to any weapon or object in the environment, such as a stick, focus on striking your opponent's knife hand first before moving in with a strike to a vital target such as the head or knee. The moment you hurt his hand and prevent him from using it against you is the time to seize the initiative and the superior position. Going for your opponent's knife hand first also allows you to stay out of reach of the knife.

Finally, to utilize the strengths of superior positioning, you must detect the threat before it is too late. If the knife attack seems to come out of nowhere and is suddenly upon you, there is probably little you can do before getting cut. Although knife defense is not a duel or sparring match, you can occasionally train as if it were a sparring match to keep you honest about the dangers of the blade. But understand that for training purposes, once the knife cuts to a valid target, the fight is over.

This U.S. Marine deflecting the knife, simultaneously gains the superior position toward his opponent's back, which also gives him several opportunities to end the fight with a strike or takedown. Note, however, that his opponent still has control of the knife. Image source: United States Marine Corps, reproduced under Wikimedia Commons license.

BLOCKING AND DEFLECTING AN ATTACK

When defending against a knife, your highest priority is to avoid getting cut. When blocking a knife attack, your block must be strong enough to stop the attacker. This may seem obvious; however, training partners who are too cooperative may give you a false sense of security. Using only one hand may not be enough. Try to reinforce your block with your other hand, with the momentum of your body, or with some sort of shield (a book or your jacket, for example). You can train with realistic speed and power by using forearm pads in order to avoid bruising your own or your partner's arm when exercising strong blocks repeatedly.

Blocking also involves more than stopping the attack. An immediate counterstrike should end the fight or at least derail your opponent. What types of strikes are good for this purpose? You can certainly use any strike thrown with power to the head, including clenched and open fist strikes. If you are holding the outside position (away from the opponent's centerline or slightly toward his or her back), a knee strike to the midsection or groin will prove relatively easy to throw, and will at least stall the opponent's momentum long enough to allow you an opportunity to wrest the knife from him or pursue the fight with additional strikes or unbalancing moves.

How realistic is your follow-up strike or kick? If you throw a front kick to the midsection, for example, will it move your opponent to the rear? If he still has the knife, you may be in renewed danger because you just gave him time to recover his momentum. If you throw a knee strike instead, and particularly if you hold the outside position, you may be in better range to pursue a disarming technique without placing yourself in the path of the knife a second time. Think about this: When disarming or defending against a knife, remaining in body-to-body contact with your opponent may minimize the risk of the knife being used against you after your initial block, strike, kick, or trap.

Make sure that your defensive strike or kick is logical. If you use a kick to defend against a knife attack, unless you can use a deceptive move to set it up, you may still risk getting cut. Image source: Martina Sprague.

When blocking a knife attack, what part of your opponent's arm should you block? Blocking high on his arm may allow the knife to extend beyond the block where it can still reach you. Blocking close to the knife, by contrast, may cause you to miss and get cut. Look to your empty-hand martial art for answers. If you block to the inside of the arm, it is generally better to block to the forearm below the elbow and near the wrist, because it prevents the opponent from bending his arm and still reaching you with the knife. If you block to the outside of the arm, it may be better to block above the elbow, because it places you close to the adversary and in position to follow with a strike, unbalancing move, or disarming attempt without placing yourself in the path of the knife.

Don't allow your opponent's knife hand to cross your body. If he uses a diagonal inward slash with his right hand and you block to the inside of his arm, his arm is to the left of your body. Keep it there. If he uses a diagonal outward slash with his right hand, and you block to the outside of his arm, his arm is to the right of your body. Keep it there.

Should you intercept and grab the arm instead of blocking? This would potentially give you greater control and knowledge of the precise location of the knife. Remember that a knife is most dangerous when in motion. An advantage of grabbing is that you seize your opponent's mobility; he can't simply withdraw the knife and attack anew. A simple block, by contrast, although it stops motion momentarily, does little to control the threat.

However, although you can attempt to intercept and grab the arm instead of blocking, it can prove difficult in the heat of battle where the smallest misjudgment or slip will mean a cut. If your grab requires two hands, you will also tie up your own hands momentarily and be unable to throw a counterstrike. If you do manage to intercept or grab your opponent's knife-wielding hand or arm, do not let go. Train with a partner using proper intent to learn whether or not you can grab and control his arm. Make sure you understand what it takes. Are you strong enough to use your planned defense? Are your hands large enough to control your opponent successfully?

If you do get a grip on your opponent's attacking arm, you must act immediately. Delaying a counterattack gives him an opportunity to wrestle out of the hold. A delay of even a second may prove detrimental. Before going for a disarming attempt, hurt your opponent enough to prevent him from striking you with the knife. If the encounter becomes a fight for the knife, the stronger person may ultimately win. If you hurt him enough, you may not even need to go for a disarming attempt. How do you hurt him enough? By striking his eyes and blinding him, for example, or by striking him hard in the throat, or by breaking his knee or ankle. One of the best counterattacks may be a violent throw. When losing his balance, his focus will shift away from the knife and toward his need to catch himself.

When deflecting rather than blocking a knife attack, deflecting horizontally is generally better than deflecting vertically. Deflecting the attack horizontally moves the knife away from your body's boundaries in the shortest line. Deflecting vertically, by contrast, moves the knife along the centerline of your body and places you in greater danger of getting cut, through the greater area the knife covers. However, it may also prove difficult to detect the angle of attack. If the adversary is at least reasonably well trained, he will not swing wide but can change the knife's trajectory with a minor motion of the wrist.

Train for precision. Engage in enough partner practice that you learn to estimate the distance from the knife to the target, so that you can recognize your safety zone. When deflecting an attack in training, do so with full determination. A deflective move, too, needs power and intent behind it. Since a deflection does not end a fight by itself, always have your next move in mind, and make sure that it is executed decisively as well.

Thus whether you block or parry (deflect the attack), your mind is on taking your opponent out or neutralizing the threat right away. Under no circumstances should you give him a second chance to harm you. This is one reason why it may prove beneficial to move to close range when blocking. When you move back and let the attack miss, the knife is still in motion. When the knife is in motion, your opponent still has control of the weapon and is still dangerous. When you block or redirect that attack and move forward, by contrast, you will stop the motion of the knife (or at least move inside of its effective range) and are more likely to gain the fraction of a second you need to neutralize the threat. If you have access to a stronger weapon than your fist (knife, club, gun, for example), you might use the moment of first touch (the moment you block or deflect the attack) to deploy this weapon. For example, block and deploy your knife, and attack. Or redirect the attack, strike your opponent, and then deploy your knife and attack.

IS SAFETY IN DISTANCE OR CLOSENESS?

Before we move forward with some knife defense exercises, it is in place to talk about distance awareness and control. The worst position as a defender facing a knife-wielding opponent is at the tip or along the cutting edge of the blade. If you can distance yourself enough to get away entirely, then safety is in distance. If not, safety is more likely in closeness.

There are two types of attacks to consider: the stab and the slash. There are also essentially two ways to defend against a knife attack: You can block or deflect the knife wielding arm, or you can attack the person, generally his balance. Blocking or deflecting the arm may work if you have the ability and determination to move in with an explosive counterstrike. Attacking the person instead of the arm gives you the benefit of taking your adversary's balance. Keep in mind that your attacker, if intent on harming you, will likely use multiple cuts or slashes as opposed to a single attack. Succeeding with a block may not be enough to stave off future attacks. Disturbing his balance buys you time.

You also have several other options when choosing your defense. For instance: To defend against a slash, move in and block to the inside of the arm. A wide swing will prove easier to block than a tight slash; however, if you detect the threat in time and decide to use this type of defense, a double forearm block may prove useful through the strength it provides. When you have blocked the attack successfully, remember to follow up with a strike intended to end or at least stall the fight long enough to render the opponent harmless through other moves. If you are skilled at balance manipulation; for example, if you have studied judo or jujutsu extensively, or if you are a trained wrestler, you can also proceed with a forward hip throw by grabbing the opponent's arm, staying close to his body, and turning to face the same direction he is while throwing him forward over your hip. Don't let go of his arm when he hits the ground. This is a good time to proceed with a disarming technique.

A wide swing is easier to detect and defend against than a tight slash. A trained knife fighter will likely not use a wide swing. However, when first starting out training in knife defense basics, you might ask your partner to exaggerate the moves until you develop timing and ability to seize the initiative. Image source: Martina Sprague.

An alternative when defending against a slash is to avoid the attack initially by moving slightly to the rear. But your timing must be good. Your opponent will now miss and, if slashing toward his centerline, will end up with his back turned slightly toward you. He may now attempt to reverse the direction of the slash. But you hold the superior position and can move to close range, block the attack to his outside arm, and counter with one of several strikes; for example, a knee to his knee joint, a knee to his groin or midsection, an uppercut to his jaw under his knife-wielding arm, or a rearward sweep or head takedown.

These examples demonstrate options for defending against a well-communicated attack, where there is little doubt what type of move your adversary will use. If he starts to slash wildly left and right while moving toward you, by contrast, it is unlikely that you can avoid the attack. If you can't distance yourself entirely, you must step forward to smother the attack, preferably by blocking to the outside of his arm to gain superior positioning. Remaining close enough for body contact to occur, and blocking to the outside of the arm and above the elbow, makes it difficult for the opponent to reach you with the edge or point of the weapon. Follow up with a strong strike to a vulnerable target that will end the fight. If you are a good grappler, a neck takedown to the rear may prove possible. When your opponent hits the ground, retain control of his arm until you can take the weapon from him.

A natural tendency when faced with a knife-wielding assailant is to raise the arms in front of your face. Although this move may allow you to protect your neck, you may also expose your arms, wrists, or hands to cuts. Your main focus in training, however, is to condition yourself to take the offensive rather than defensive approach even in empty-hand self-defense. If you are not able to preempt an attack, strive to seize the initiative as quickly as possible. Ideally, place your opponent in a situation where he feels as though he is losing control, by moving to close range as soon as possible after your first successful defensive move. If you have an opportunity to launch a preemptive attack, when is the best time to do so? Can you distract your opponent, for example, through something you say, and attack when his focus diverts for a second?

Although safety may be in closeness, you must also consider where your opponent's greatest strength is. For example, if he executes a downward overhead stab with the knife in the reverse grip, you will have greater chance of success if you block the swing prior to his arm reaching the 90-degree angle. If his arm goes past 90-degrees, he can rely on previously established momentum. The knife will also be closer to you, so a successful defense at this point is more difficult.

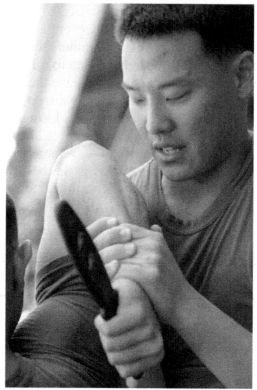

A defense against a downward overhead stab works best if you block before the opponent's arm goes past the horizontal position, or 90-degree angle. To continue with a disarming technique or takedown, you must get to very close range, where you can rely on the strength of your body to subdue the adversary, as demonstrated in this defense by a U.S. Marine against a knife-wielding opponent. Image source: United States Marine Corps, reproduced under Wikimedia Commons license.

BASIC KNIFE DEFENSE EXERCISES

Experiment with different attack scenarios with a partner when practicing empty-hand defenses against knife attacks. Explore how to execute a block, seize the initiative, and counterstrike against overhead/icepick attacks, straight stabs, and inward and outward slashes with the knife in the forward grip. We will look at reverse grip tactics, dynamic defenses involving takedowns, and knife threats involving coercion in Book 7 of the *Knife Training Methods and Techniques for Martial Artists* series. An experienced defender might also drop below the attack and go for a leg takedown. For now, try the following:

Exercise 1

When experimenting with knife defense basics, ask yourself: What does it take? For example, what does it take to avoid the first cut? What does it take to buy three seconds of time to escape? What does it take to unbalance a bigger assailant armed with a knife in the heat of battle? What does it take to survive a knife attack, when your opponent has taken you down and is sitting on you?

Exercise 2

A good way to train in order to develop an understanding of the options available to you is to observe your partner as he or she initiates an attack against you, but without allowing the knife to touch you. Have your partner face you and initiate an overhead or straight stab or slash, halting the movement of the knife before it makes contact. Consider what type of defense you might use. Repeat the exercise with your partner attacking from the side, again without allowing the knife to touch you. Use your peripheral vision to prepare a defensive move.

Exercise 3

When practicing with a partner, start by blocking or parrying a single stab or slash. Once you get a feel for the timing, practice blocking or parrying two successive stabs or slashes. Increase the speed of the attack and add a counterstrike after your initial block or parry.

Exercise 4

When defending against an overhead stab with the knife, block or deflect the attack with one hand, immediately following with a strike with your other hand or a kick designed to end the fight. There should be a split second between your moves. The block or deflection gives you a feel for your opponent's timing and ensures that you won't get cut. The counterstrike prevents your opponent from capitalizing on his failed attack, for example, by taking advantage of the momentum of your deflective move.

Exercise 5

Simply knowing that you should distance yourself from

an attack will probably not help much. You must also experiment to find out what it takes. Try staying away from somebody intent on attacking you with a knife. It's not easy. Your range will quickly go from long to short, and you will not have time to backpedal, sidestep, intercept, or whatever else you have learned in martial arts class. Take advantage of the first opportunity to move to very close range, where you can smother your opponent, attack his vital areas, or take his balance. Attempt to gain an outside position (away from your opponent's centerline), then strike or go for the unbalancing move.

Exercise 6

Movement alone is seldom sufficient against a knife attack; that is, unless you are a much faster runner than your opponent and have unlimited space to get away. But if you are in any kind of confined area, you are not likely to get away by running. Try it with your buddies in the training hall. Arm your friend with a fake knife and see how far you get by running, and how long it takes until he cuts you. This exercise teaches you that defense is not enough, and you must assume an offensive mindset if you are to end the fight in your favor.

Exercise 7

Train from inferior positions, such as with your back against a wall or sitting down on a chair when attacked. How can your opponent restrict your moves or defensive tactics? Can he grab your clothing and manipulate the movement of your body? Also train with opponents of varying build. You will most likely find that the same type of attack is executed differently by different people. You can therefore not assume that a particular defensive move will work precisely as planned.

Exercise 8

Experiment with trapping your opponent's knife hand. If he won't let go of the knife, how can you direct the knife back toward him? Can you go with the motion? Can you use a joint lock? Can you use a joint lock and take him down while simultaneously directing the knife toward him?

Exercise 9

Explore the possibility that you will not be successful or only partially so defending against a knife attack. The moment your defense fails or nearly so, halt the exercise, acknowledge the flaws, and discuss with your partner why the defensive move failed. This exercise triggers your imagination and informs you of what you could have done to increase your success rate. Once you become aware of the fact that your defensive technique will probably have some flaws, you can establish the mindset needed not to give up and continue defending to the best of your ability, even if you get cut in the process.

Exercise 10

When you have avoided the first cut, make sure you do enough damage to force your adversary to think of defending himself rather than attacking you. The idea is to seize the initiative and cause as much chaos as possible, and not let up until you have secured your safety. For instance, after blocking the attack, strike with an open palm to the jaw, and immediately grab around your opponent's neck and throw a knee to his midsection, groin, or leg. The chaos of the move will force him to struggle to retain his wits. You may now have several options: Remove yourself from the situation, hurt him even more, or disarm him. Yes, you might take a cut to your arm in the process as your adversary struggles to get his body and mind back in balance and starts to swing wildly with the knife, but you will likely have at least a fairly good chance of saving your life. Think foremost of protecting your neck against a slash. There is also a possibility that you will not take a cut. Taking a cut is not inevitable, even though the risk is there.

A good way to train in order to develop an understanding of the options available is to observe your partner as he or she initiates an attack against you, and halts the movement of the knife before it makes contact. Image source: Martina Sprague.

EXERCISE IN FUTILITY OR GOOD SELF-DEFENSE SKILLS?

Now then that you have had some time to practice defending yourself against a knife-wielding assailant, let's recap some of the concepts we have learned and talk about the need to introduce realism into the martial arts training hall, and why, if you're not aware of the pitfalls, knife defense training may either make you overconfident (if your training partners are too cooperative) or seem like an exercise in futility (if your training partners refuse to cooperate enough).

As you go through different ways to defend against the knife, you will probably at some point ask if the defense is realistic or not. The difficult part is that we normally train with a cooperative partner, who uses a speed that we can easily intercept, and an attack that we understand and can see coming beforehand. This type of training is necessary in order to bring about understanding of how an attack can happen and the options available. It also allows us to work on timing and precision while honing our skill. But as you get better, you might question the extent to which your defenses will prove effective if the attack comes at a much greater speed than what you are used to, or with greater force. Is your block sufficient against that icepick overhead stab? Do you really have time to sidestep the attack before the knife strikes you?

Is your block sufficiently powerful against a downward stab with the full weight of the body behind it? How can you block the attack while simultaneously moving away from the knife's trajectory and to the superior position toward your opponent's back? Image source: Martina Sprague.

Effective self-defense comprises two parts: technique and strategy. This is one reason why cardio-karate classes, for example, are useless for self-defense, even though they often claim to teach you "valuable self-defense skills." The kicks and punches you throw are worthless if you don't also learn the strategy: how a self-defense situation develops, how to enter into battle, how you will react to getting hit, how to use your techniques in combinations while defending yourself, how to angle out after executing offense, and the list goes on. Self-defense is not a mindless act.

Yet in empty-hand practice we often fail to realize how serious an attack can be. Gloves are used, punches are pulled, and you will never get a real sense for the damage you could suffer. When starting out with knife defense basics in the training hall, and once you are past the static stage where every move is predictable and slow, your practice partner should attack with reasonable intent to land a stab or slash.

Although you may have a deep theoretical understanding of a technique, once your training partner starts attacking with speed and determination, many of your previously learned moves may be difficult to pull off. Techniques often sound good in theory but prove impractical in a real attack, mostly because of differences in speed, and also because of deception. To gain further understanding of how valuable your theories are and where they are lacking, it is crucial to experiment with realistic speed (using dull training knives and appropriate protective gear, of course). Live partners rather than training dummies are crucial to providing near realistic intensity and stress. Training with partners also helps you develop a sense for distance, angles, and timing.

Practicing knife defense with fake knives but realistic speed also teaches you about your reflexes and fighting spirit, and informs you of how well you control your emotions when under pressure to perform. It could be a humbling experience, because it exposes you to the realities of combat. It teaches you how careful you must be when guarding your life, even if you have decades of martial arts studies under your belt.

Using a weapon that is hard enough to be felt without

injuring you, or using paint to show a cut, will make you disciplined in your training and give you a quick indication of what you can and cannot do at your particular level of skill. Soft foam rubber knives tend to make us overconfident, however. A semi-legitimate threat will give you more respect for the weapon; it will teach you to act with determination and explosiveness; it will teach you to find your window of opportunity and act on it.

Consistent training to maintain physical fitness and getting used to being manhandled slightly (under the oversight of a professional instructor), will further help you absorb the power of an attack and recover from sustained injures quicker. You will also increase your pain threshold, until a little bit of pain no longer causes you to freeze or turn away from the attack. Some people deal with pain better than others, but all of us can train to become stronger.

Although it may initially seem as though the defensive techniques you have learned in your empty-hand martial art are exceedingly difficult to pull off against an attacker intent on harming you, with sufficient practice you will gain confidence using your previously learned empty-hand martial arts skills successfully. But remember that no matter how skilled you are, when going empty handed against a bladed weapon, the odds are not in your favor.

CONCLUDING THOUGHTS

The primary purpose of any defensive technique is to avoid getting struck. However, if this is as far as you go, you will still risk subsequent attacks. A defensive technique is therefore incomplete until you have countered with a strike or move that renders your opponent harmless. The ideal defensive technique places you in position to execute a counterattack without exposing you to additional danger.

Historical Gem: Early nineteenth century Prussian soldier and military theorist Carl von Clausewitz stressed that defense as the stronger form of war, because it is generally "easier to hold ground than to take it." See Carl von Clausewitz, On War, edited and translated by Michael Howard and Peter Paret (Princeton, NJ: Princeton University Press, 1976), 357. However, he also explained that it is impossible to rely on defense alone. In short, defense must have purpose; defense must be offensive, for example, through surprise or superior positioning. Defense has several aims: To protect you from harm, to destroy the enemy's ability to fight (for example, by tiring the enemy), and to create offense. Defense executed with correct timing will interfere with the opponent's offense and cause "friction" that may deny him the victory. Defense is thus not merely passive, but consists of two parts: avoiding or blocking the attack and counterattacking. The changeover from defense to offense should happen as soon as the defender has determined that it will benefit him. The counterattack is absolutely necessary, because without it you will be unable to pursue the objective.

A problem inherent to practicing defensive techniques step by step is the assumption that these defenses will work. We fail to let the attack continue to conclusion as it would in a real scenario, and fail to explore what to do when we realize that the defensive technique has failed. I recommend that you educate yourself on the principles of knife defense and the situations that could happen, and then find techniques that work for you based on your training and research.

However, you must also have some idea of what to do ahead of time. Adapting to the situation as it unfolds sounds nice, but will not necessarily work in the chaos of the attack. Why? Because there may not be enough time to see how the situation unfolds. You may only have one or two seconds. You will not be facing your opponent in a duel.

There are thus two ways you can train: You can decide which techniques you are going to use, and train your body and mind until you get comfortable with these techniques; or you can explore what types of movements are naturally suited to your body type in particular, and develop your techniques around these moves.

Once you have decided on a training regimen, you can set up different scenarios:

1. The surprise attack where you don't know that you have been cut until after it's over, and that leaves you little or no room and time to defend yourself no matter how skilled a martial artist you are.

2. The attack where you know that you are in danger and the situation is tense also for your adversary. This type of attack may allow you to distract your opponent, or strike to a vulnerable target that may give you options for a successful defense even if you get cut in the process.

3. The coercive attack where your opponent does not want to kill you but wants something from you, such as a material object, your body (as in kidnapping or rape), or some knowledge that you possess.

Each scenario gives you different opportunities for defending empty handed against the knife. You can therefore not look at a defensive technique in the training hall and instantly determine whether or not it will work. Many issues factor into the equation. As martial artists, we can discuss, analyze, and practice different techniques and scenarios to discover where the strengths and weaknesses of each technique lie. If you can limit your choices of defenses to just a few, it will probably benefit you in the long run. For example, recognize that anytime you end up to the outside of your opponent's body or away from his centerline, certain techniques are available to you that are not as easily available if you end up to the inside of his body or along his centerline.

Is there such a thing as a superior technique? Not necessarily. A common saying in the martial arts is that the best technique is the one you can use when you need it. If you want insurance against getting hurt in a fight, you need to attack from a distance with a firearm. If you are within range to touch your opponent, he is also within range to touch you. Will this bit of knowledge make you any less of a martial artist? Of course not. The martial arts are not about securing an escape every time, but about recognizing danger or the breeding grounds for violence and ultimately saving your life. This is why it is traditionally noble to leave the scene when things begin to boil. Unless you must stay in order to save others, it is better to leave and appear a coward than to fight and appear macho. The fact that you choose to leave means that you have enough insight into fighting to know that there is a price to pay in every fight. More often than not, the price is not worth it.

Knife Defense Dynamics

Book 7

Knife Training Methods and Techniques for Martial Artists

by Martina Sprague

TABLE OF CONTENTS

Introduction	55
Brief History	58
Lesson Objectives	61
Dynamic Knife Defense Concepts	62
Avoiding the First Cut	65
Simple Defense and Disarming Practice	70
Some Ways to Control the Opponent	73
Taking the Opponent's Balance	77
On the Ground	84
The Knife as a Weapon of Coercion	92
Neutralizing the Threat	99
Additional Thoughts on Knife Defense Dynamics	104
Understanding Pain	109

INTRODUCTION

Weapons extend your reach and are designed to be used from a distance. Good control of distance further allows a knife-wielding assailant to reach you while depriving you of the ability to reach him. The best time to defend against a weapon attack is therefore generally when the weapon is close to the attacker's body, when he is unable to make full use of distance and reach. Moreover, a knife (or other weapon with reach such as a club) has more power and is more difficult to defend against when in motion. This is one reason why defenses against knife attacks are often practiced stationary or in slow motion, rather than at full speed in the training hall. This is necessary for learning proper mechanics of technique, before you can learn proper timing.

With the foregoing in mind, initiating your defense when the weapon is close to the attacker's body, for example, by pinning his arm or disturbing his balance, may prevent him from setting the weapon in motion. Simultaneously you must recognize that the long range capabilities of the knife in your opponent's hand may prevent you from achieving an advantageous position close to his body. Executing a sound defense in response to a knife attack may prove more complicated than initially thought.

Let me reiterate that the knife is a superior weapon. It doesn't malfunction and it doesn't run out of ammunition. It can thrust and slash several times in a few seconds. When defending empty-handed against a knife-wielding opponent, you must disarm him, incapacitate him, or buy yourself enough time to flee the encounter. Martial arts techniques sometimes fail when applied in real time, because you are taught moves that require the use of fine motor skills. Rather than initiating your defense with a disarming attempt, a more practical alternative is to avoid or block the first cut and launch an immediate incapacitating technique or stunning counter-attack that buys you enough time to further incapacitate your opponent or flee the encounter. When initiating your defense, don't aim for the weapon. Aim for the person you are fighting. It is the person, primarily, who is dangerous. Hurt him first in order to disarm him later.

When discussing the knife as an equalizer in combat, we should also recognize that it is hand-to-hand combat, or close range fighting, that applies, despite the extra reach the weapon affords the assailant. A gun, for example, has great capacity to harm from a distance. If you have access to a gun, don't get so close to your opponent that you give him the option of taking the gun from you. Likewise, if your opponent has a gun and you are not within physical reach of the weapon, there is little you can do initially to defend against the attack, except trying to talk your way out of the situation. When we discuss knives, by contrast, we must recognize that, unlike the gun, the knife, much like our hands and feet, is only effective at a range where we can reach our opponent. If you are engaged in a hand-to-hand encounter when your opponent deploys a knife, the situation will immediately become dire. The moment you recognize that he has a live blade, and the moment he knows that you recognize this fact, he also knows that he has the upper hand in the fight. The knife gives him psychological power, because it is a weapon that is truly capable of inflicting severe physical damage quickly, even in the hands of an unskilled person.

As explained in Book 1, the *Knife Training Methods and Techniques for Martial Artists* series has three objectives: The first few books focus on getting to know the knife, its strengths and weaknesses, and on manipulating and using it. The next few books focus on defending against knife attacks. The last few books focus on implementing empty-hand martial arts skills into your knife training, and include scenario-based exercises intended to bring your knowledge into perspective and give you a solid understanding of your strengths and weaknesses when faced with a knife-wielding assailant. Each book starts with an introduction. You are then given the lesson objectives, along with detailed information and a number of training exercises aimed at making you physically and emotionally ready to participate in traditional martial arts demonstrations involving a knife or, if fate will have it, in a real encounter. Remember that it is your responsibility to know and comply with all federal and local laws regarding the possession and carry of edged weapons.

BRIEF HISTORY

If you have studied the previous books in the *Knife Training Methods and Techniques for Martial Artists* series, you should have a good understanding of how to deploy, manipulate, and attack with a knife by now, and therefore have a good understanding of the types of danger you are up against when facing a knife-wielding opponent empty-handed. You should also have developed some understanding of basic techniques for defending against a knife attack. When starting to train in knife defense dynamics, think beyond the initial defensive move. The first step is to avoid the attack, or ensure that neither the knife nor the opponent will touch you. But avoiding the first cut, for example, by parrying or sidestepping the strike, does not prevent your opponent from attempting a new attack. Offense must follow defense in order to secure your safety. Only offense will ultimately prevent your opponent from continuing the assault, allow you to seize the initiative, take the fight from him, and secure your safety. Only offense prevents your opponent from carrying his attack to conclusion. Executing offense immediately following defense, however, generally requires speed, excellent timing, and a willingness to press the attack. You may have to advance toward your opponent, crowd him to impair his mobility and balance, and force him to retreat.

As emphasized in Book 6 of the *Knife Training Methods and Techniques for Martial Artist* series, early nineteenth century Prussian military strategist, Carl von Clausewitz, propagated defense as the stronger form of war, because it is generally "easier to hold ground than to take it." See

Carl von Clausewitz, *On War*, edited and translated by Michael Howard and Peter Paret (Princeton, NJ: Princeton University Press, 1976), 357. However, he also pointed out that it is impossible to rely on defense alone, because there can be no "war" unless both sides agree to exchange blows. There is no contradiction in Clausewitz's view on defense. In short, defense must have purpose; defense must be offensive, for example, through surprise or superior positioning. Defense has several aims: To protect you from harm, to destroy the enemy's ability to fight (for example, by tiring the enemy), and to create offense. As early as in Classical times, a shield wall was used to advance on the enemy on the battlefield. The shields not only protected against the enemy's weapons, but also allowed the bearers to force the enemy into retreat. What should be learned from war history is that defense executed with correct timing will interfere with the enemy's offense and cause "friction" that may deny him the victory.

When practicing dynamic knife defenses, keep in mind that your opponent will likely attempt more than a single stab or slash. If he is intent on attacking you, he will stab or slash several times in rapid succession while moving forward. This will complicate matters and prevent you from using techniques that require fine motor skills; for example, techniques that rely on intercepting or catching the attack and applying a joint lock. You must generally precede a disarming technique with a move that uses gross motor skills. This could be a forceful double forearm block, followed by a strong strike to a primary target such as the eyes. But if you fumble with your defense, you risk getting stabbed multiple times.

Historical Gem: Successful knife defenses depend on your ability to detect danger and see the attack coming. But even then, according to British soldier and hand-to-hand combat expert, William Ewart Fairbairn (1885-1960), "In close-quarters fighting there is no more deadly weapon than the knife. An entirely unarmed man has no certain defense against it, and, further, merely the sudden flashing of a knife is frequently enough to strike fear into your opponent, causing him to lose confidence and surrender." See Captain W. E. Fairbairn, *Get Tough: How to Win in Hand-to-Hand Fighting* (Boulder, CO: Paladin Press, 1979), 96.

Those who become experts in knife attacks and defenses are typically soldiers or criminals. But if you're not a soldier and not unfortunate enough to have to get rid of a sentry at night, and if you're not a criminal, then how do you learn to fight and defend against a knife? As a martial artist, you may never consider yourself a true knife fighting expert, simply because your training environment doesn't allow for deadly attacks and defenses. However, once you have spent time practicing in the training hall and begun to understand the dynamics of a knife attack and how a knife-wielding opponent might use his weapon against you, you will grow as a martial artist and gain confidence in your defensive capabilities in edged weapon encounters. As you study the techniques in this book, remember that they constitute suggestions; they are not meant to constitute the only ways in which you can defend against a knife attack.

LESSON OBJECTIVES

Upon completion of this lesson, you should:

1. Have acquired an understanding of your options when faced with a knife-wielding assailant

2. Have had some opportunity to practice different ways to control the adversary rather than the knife

3. Have gained insights into simple disarming techniques, balance manipulation, and knife defenses from the ground

4. Have developed an understanding of the difference between an opponent intent on killing with the knife, and one using the knife as a weapon of coercion

5. Have started to practice different ways to neutralize the threat

6. Have had an opportunity to explore the dangers of knife defense dynamics and how pain might affect your defensive capabilities

DYNAMIC KNIFE DEFENSE CONCEPTS

Bruce Lee (1940-1973), perhaps the leading martial artist of all time, emphasized formlessness, or the art of no art. Formlessness means flexibility to adapt to changing circumstances, or to paraphrase: answering questions as they are posed and not before they are asked. Others take a different view and argue that success comes by creating the fewest number of choices possible, and by bringing yourself to a position of familiarity under stress, where you recognize options you can use in each scenario. It is not necessary to learn a hundred different defenses against a hundred different attacks. By recognizing the common denominators, you can develop just a handful of defenses that work against most attacks. For example, every time you parry and move away from your opponent's centerline (to the outside of his arm), you have a rear takedown or hip throw available regardless of how the attack was initiated. In knife training, you might be defending against a straight stab, or an overhead icepick stab, or a slash. In each of these attacks, once you achieve an outside position (away from your opponent's centerline and toward his back), you have a rear takedown or hip throw available.

The outside defensive position (away from the opponent's centerline) is generally superior to the inside defensive position (toward your opponent's centerline). But gaining the outside position by parrying the initial attack does not relieve you of the necessity to act with immediate offense. When he misses with the attack, your opponent's first thought is to make a new attempt. Don't lose your window of opportunity by failing to act.

Thus with the foregoing in mind, and since it is difficult to defend successfully against a knife-wielding assailant intent on harming you, learning a few useful principles that can be applied in several possible scenarios may ultimately take you further than memorizing a number of specific and complex techniques. Defending against a knife attack involves more than evading or blocking the first cut. The knife is a highly versatile weapon, in many ways even more versatile than a handgun. The knife is lightweight and maneuverable with either hand. It can be operated in tight motions within a small area, and it is capable of producing several cuts per second. When practicing dynamic defenses against knife attacks, your goal is to remove your opponent's ability to attack rather than remove his weapon. Your defense may include moves designed to injure his hands or legs, or taking his balance. Remember that if he loses his foundation, he can't move, and can therefore not fight.

A defensive technique can thus prove simpler to execute if you think of the end result rather than the means. What would happen, for example, if your instructor simply told you to "avoid the attack"? How you respond will certainly depend on the moves that are comfortable to you and with which you are most familiar. But in general, you would forget about using fine motor skills initially. Engaging in complicated joint or finger locks will prove difficult even if you are well-versed in these techniques. The problem is that the adrenaline you experience in a real fight, where your life is threatened with a bladed weapon, is difficult to duplicate in the martial arts training hall. A good way to start is by focusing on developing a response that buys you time until you can engage your adversary in a disarming technique. Before proceeding to learn about dynamic knife defenses, ponder the following concepts:

1. As discussed in previous books of the *Knife Training Methods and Techniques for Martial Artists* series, you must be aware of your opponent's hands at all times, because this is where the weapon is.

2. When the knife attack is inevitable, it is often better to initiate than wait for your opponent to attack and then react, because when you seize the initiative, you eliminate (or nearly so) the risk of being taken by surprise. When you initiate, you also dictate the fight and force the adversary into a reactive state of mind.

3. If possible, force your opponent to retreat while you control his attacking arm. This will complicate his ability to launch an effective attack against you.

4. Attempt to steal your opponent's balance as soon as possible after the initial tie-up, or when you first make physical contact with any part of his body.

As you implement these concepts in practice, keep in mind that if your first attempt at controlling the attacker fails, you will be at increased risk of getting cut, or in worst case scenario, losing the battle entirely.

AVOIDING THE FIRST CUT

What are your options, then, when defending against a knife attack? You can try a parry or block followed by a joint control hold. But a joint lock is difficult to pull off when your opponent has size, speed, momentum, and determination.

1. Start by exploring your chances of avoiding the initial cut by catching your opponent's wrist with both hands and directing the knife away from you.

2. Take a superior position preferably toward his back to avoid the knife.

3. Attempt to take him to the ground rather than disarming him. Do not go down with him. If you have difficulty taking your opponent down from the wrist catch, use your whole bodyweight to force him off balance.

4. Once he hits the ground, an option is to release your grip and run even if he still has the knife. It will take some time and effort for him to get back on his feet, and he may not have the desire to chase you down and continue the assault at this point.

If your opponent is big and strong, you might have to use a softening technique before you can neutralize the attack. The same principle applies to joint control holds. A softening technique splits your opponent's focus and increases your probability to succeed with your defense or disarming technique. What type of softening technique can you use before attempting a disarm? Explore a kick to the knee first, before moving in for the disarm. Your opponent's focus is on the knife in his hand, and any attack to a low target will likely split his focus.

Caution: If you fake a strike to draw a reaction from your opponent before closing distance and taking his balance or disarming him, keep in mind that he will probably be quite tense. He knows that he cannot afford to lose the knife. If you fake a strike you may not get the expected flinch reaction, but might trigger a full attack from your adversary instead.

When your opponent is past the threat phase and has launched the attack, his intent on killing you is clear. His full focus is on reaching you with the knife. He is no longer thinking about how to protect his own sensitive targets, such as the throat, eyes, groin, and knees. If you manage to avoid the first cut, your next step should be attacking the inherently weak areas of his body. Aim for his eyes or drive your foot into his knee. Remember that the knife is your opponent's strength, and it is better to attack his weakness than his strength.

Trying to disarm an opponent when his knife is in motion is highly unrealistic. The risk of getting cut is much too great when you rely on fine motor skills and are under a great deal of stress besides. You must place him in an inferior position prior to attempting to disarm him, preferably in a position where he is more concerned with his own pain or safety than with cutting you. For example, you might try to disarm him after you have taken him to the ground and have full control of his knife arm; after you have delivered a painful strike to his groin, ribs, throat, or eyes; or after you have broken a bone or torn a ligament in his fingers, elbow, knee, or ankle.

If your opponent uses a roundhouse motion in a stabbing or slashing attack with the knife, you have several options. For example, you can block to the inside of the attack by using a single or double forearm block. If using a double forearm block, your body will be turned to the side toward the knife arm. A good follow-up technique might be a reverse elbow strike to the neck or head. If using a single forearm block with the arm closest to the knife, your body will be turned forward a bit more, giving you the option to follow with a straight palm strike to your opponent's head. If the knife strike comes low toward your midsection, however, a forearm block is more difficult to use. You might try to keep your arms very close to your body and your head down to protect your neck, while swiftly moving forward and inside of the arc of the knife. The knife will strike the air behind your back. You might take a surface cut on your back, but without any real power behind it. Use your body momentum to push your opponent off balance and follow with a strong palm strike to his head. You can also wrap your arm over his knife arm above the elbow and take him down.

When defending against a knife attack, whether from the outside or inside position, as seen here, you must immediately follow with a strike designed to hurt or at least stun your opponent. Defense and offense therefore occur within the same move. Image source: Martina Sprague.

What about kicking the knife from your opponent's hand? Some hold the view that such a move would require too much precision to prove effective, and that it is also dangerous because you risk getting cut along your leg. But at least consider this type of defense if you are wearing heavy boots. A good kick can help you maintain distance, stun your adversary, or hurt him even if you don't disarm him, thus buying you time to move in with an unbalancing technique. An outside crescent kick, using the side of your foot, might prove more useful than a front kick which needs more precision to execute against the knife. You might also use kicks as distractions by kicking your opponent's legs. Furthermore, some hold the view that it is difficult to throw high kicks in street clothes. In my view, however, blue jeans are generally soft and flexible enough to allow you to kick at least chin height without difficulty, and certainly hand or weapon height.

SIMPLE DEFENSE AND DISARMING PRACTICE

Now, then, before proceeding with balance manipulation, let's start with some simple defenses and disarming techniques that you may already be familiar with. Feel free to change these suggestions by implementing techniques that are specific to your martial art. But try to remain within the basic principles of dynamic knife defenses, which stress seizing the initiative by hurting or stunning your adversary before attempting to disarm him. For the purpose of this exercise, we will assume that your opponent is right-handed.

Simple defense and disarming technique against forward grip thrust

1. When the opponent thrusts with the knife, step to the side, preferably away from his centerline, and pivot your body off the attack line. Simultaneously block with both forearms to the back of his arm.

2. Grab the attacker's wrist with your right hand, simultaneously striking him in the face with a left back elbow.

3. Now that you have executed your initial defense and hurt him, bring your left hand to his wrist and take him to the ground by applying a wrist lock. Be aware of the location of the weapon at all times.

4. Use his elbow and wrist as leverage points to turn him to an inferior position on his stomach. You can now

disarm him and eliminate the threat by using the knife against him, or by breaking his wrist or elbow, rendering him incapable of further offense.

Simple defense and disarming technique against forward grip slash

1. When the opponent slashes with the knife in a wide arc toward you, move inside of the attack. Although moving toward the centerline poses a different set of risks than maintaining the outside position, a benefit is that you have easy access to multiple targets with your elbows and knees.

2. Block the attack with a double forearm block to the inside of the opponent's arm. Grab his wrist with your left hand, simultaneously striking him in the face with a right back elbow. As you can see, in addition to working along your opponent's centerline, this technique is the mirror image of the previous one.

3. Now that you have hurt your opponent, turn to face the same direction he is. Maintain control of his knife hand.

4. Place his straight arm, elbow down, over your shoulder. Disarm your opponent by hyper-extending his elbow against your shoulder. You can also break his elbow or damage the ligaments at this time to prevent further attack. If you are skilled at throws, use his arm for leverage and throw him forward over your shoulder.

A takedown or throw can be executed by placing your opponent's arm over your shoulder, elbow down, and using it as leverage. If he resists the throw, he risks having his arm broken. Image source: Judcosta, reproduced under Wikimedia Commons license.

Think about this: When practicing defenses against knife attacks in the training hall, and after you have gained some familiarity with the techniques, ask your practice partner to resist your defense. If the fight were for real, both you and your opponent would likely be quite tense. When adding chaos to your defensive drills, how likely are you to succeed? How effective are your knife defenses or disarming techniques when both you and your opponent are in motion? When your opponent realizes he is about to be defeated, he will do everything in his power to regain his edge. He knows that if you defeat him, you might also gain access to the knife and kill him.

SOME WAYS TO CONTROL THE OPPONENT

As learned in Book 3 of the *Knife Training Methods and Techniques for Martial Artists* series, a knife is most dangerous when in motion, because this is when it is most difficult to intercept and control. The knife is a weapon of reach, and the best time to defend against it is generally when it is close to the attacker's body. But when the attacker's arm is close to his body, he can also use the knife in quick and elusive moves. It is therefore a good idea to strive to control the opponent, rather than attempt to disarm him initially. If possible, intercept his arm close to his body, preferably above the elbow where there is less movement and greater potential for control.

If he extends the knife toward you at the initiation of the attack, as practiced in the previous exercises, a possible defense is to sidestep the attack and intercept and grab his arm. Be prepared to use both hands for a strong grip. Your opponent will likely tense the moment you grab him. But this could also benefit you by improving your chances of controlling his arm and therefore the rest of his body. However, you must be mentally and physically prepared to act immediately to avoid using strength against strength. The quicker you proceed with an unbalancing move, the better. For example, use his arm as a lever to take his balance to the rear. Or grab his arm with both hands as you turn your back toward him, facing the same direction he is. Place his arm over your shoulder, elbow down, and exert stress on the elbow to get him to release the knife. You can also throw him forward over your shoulder from this position. Once he loses his balance, he is no longer an immediate threat to you, even if he has control of the knife.

A forceful push to the shoulder of your opponent's knife-wielding arm can stop an attack, but this type of defense works best against a roundhouse-type wide swing. You must reach his shoulder before the knife reaches you. The moment he staggers from your push, proceed with a technique designed to hurt or stun him further. Try a kick with your shin straight up between his legs. You have now established a situation where you might be able to proceed with a disarming technique. If the attack is a straight stab, by contrast, the shoulder push will prove difficult and quite a bit riskier, because you will be moving directly into the path of the knife.

If the adversary attacks in an overhead stab with the knife in the icepick grip, you might try a block or parry while moving to the outside of his arm. Immediately follow with an eye gouge or palm strike to the jaw or forehead. When his neck snaps back, run. If you strike his jaw or nose instead of his forehead, and he has a strong neck, the force of your strike may prove insufficient for giving you the time you need to distance yourself. Striking high to the forehead gives you greater leverage, because the forehead is farther than the jaw from the axis of rotation (the neck).

When working on defending against the icepick stab in training, pay particularly attention to the importance of timing. You must react and move forward the moment you sense that the attack is inevitable. If the knife has fallen through the apex (highest point) of the arc, you are better off trying to distance yourself from the trajectory of the swing, and proceed with a strike, kick, or controlling technique when the knife has missed its target and your opponent is concerned about recovering his composure.

If the knife has fallen through the apex, as seen here, defending with a block, controlling technique, and takedown may prove difficult, because at this point the adversary has his or her full weight behind the technique. This is one reason why timing your defense to the opponent's attack is crucial. Image source: Martina Sprague.

You might also try a choke and takedown as part of a defensive technique aimed at controlling an opponent attacking you with the knife in the icepick grip. Parry or block the attack and step to the outside of his arm, immediately wrapping your arm around his neck and taking him down to the rear. This takedown works well even if you are unable to step behind his leg. Remain close to your opponent. There should be no space between your bodies. You can control his knife hand by pressing your upper body into his upper arm.

If the adversary places the knife against your back or side of body, a quick pivot with your elbow knocking his arm away from your body may help you escape the initial threat. But you must follow up immediately, because you have technically not hurt him yet, and the knife is therefore still in his control. The fact that your opponent has a lethal weapon and you don't, gives him strength and mental superiority, even if his initial attempt to attack failed.

If you fail to control the knife when moving away after a close encounter, be particularly keen on preventing the knife from crossing in front of your body. When distancing yourself from the attack, do so by moving away from the trajectory of the knife.

TAKING THE OPPONENT'S BALANCE

Now that you have some idea of how to use basic knife defense principles, including seizing the initiative and controlling the opponent, let's continue by examining a few ways in which you may take your opponent's balance.

When your initial defense consists of controlling the adversary's arm, relying on strikes or kicks may prove counterproductive, and a move that takes his balance may be better. However, a slight increase in distance, for example, by setting your weight over your rear foot, may allow you to throw a strike or kick as a softening technique without sacrificing control, even if you are very close to the adversary and have already pinned his knife-wielding hand. Regardless of whether your martial art focuses on strikes and kicks or control holds and grappling, do not relinquish control you have achieved simply for the benefit of staying within the confines of your art.

Attacking your opponent's knife hand is a good option when closing distance, particularly if you, too, have a knife or other weapon that you can use for striking. If you are already at close range when the threat gets serious, attacking a vital target such as the eyes or throat might be better. If you are very close to your opponent, you might look at trapping his knife arm with a tight overhook (hooking his arm with yours above the elbow) to gain control and prevent the knife from cutting you.

Overhooking the opponent's arm above the elbow places

you at very close range where you can take advantage of the strength in your body. But before you do so, you should attempt to hurt him with a strong strike to decrease the risk of the encounter turning into a struggle for control of the knife. An elbow strike to his head while you retain control of his arm can prove devastating. As soon as you land the strike, move one leg behind your opponent's leg until you are hip to hip, and then throw him backwards to the ground. The moment he lands, you have the option of letting go of his arm and running away (it will take him a while to recover from the throw), or proceed with a disarming technique and additional offense, if deemed necessary.

One of the simpler throws is the rearward hip throw. By placing your hip against the adversary's and stepping behind his leg to control his foundation, you can manipulate his balance with relative ease. Image source: Judcosta, reproduced under Wikimedia Commons license.

If you manage to get behind your opponent before gaining control of his knife arm, you might take him down by kicking to the back of his knee and simultaneously pulling his upper body or head to the rear, for example, by cupping his chin with both hands. Your objective is to drive your foot into the back of the knee joint, and keep driving until his knee hits the ground. Cupping his chin with your hands and pulling his upper body toward you will aid the technique by taking his balance and preventing him from stepping forward. With his weight to the rear and his upper body outside of his center of gravity, his only choice is to take a step back to maintain balance. But driving your foot into the back of his knee will prevent this.

Let's look at two additional ways in which you can take the opponent's balance as defense against a knife attack.

Figure-four defensive throw against the icepick overhead stab

Ideally, any defensive technique against a bladed weapon should be initiated at the earliest stage in order to thwart the attack. The figure-four defensive throw assumes that your opponent is holding the knife in the reverse grip in preparation for an overhead (icepick) stabbing attack.

1. When the adversary initiates the attack and before his hand has moved through the apex (the highest point) of the vertical arc, move forward with an upward block, meeting the momentum of your opponent's arm with yours. When practicing in the training hall, pay attention to the importance of timing and moving forward to seize

the initiative in order to intercept the attack successfully.

2. Grab his arm in the figure-four lock as you continue walking forward. Place your foot behind your opponent until you are hip to hip facing opposite directions. The success of this technique presupposes that you have some prior experience in joint locks, takedowns, and throws. Your success also depends on forcing your opponent's balance slightly to the rear of his center of gravity by immobilizing his foundation.

3. Throw your opponent rearward over your hip. Or, if you prefer, take him down by continuing walking forward and directing the motion of his knife hand toward the ground. A hip throw is more violent than a takedown, but either works as long as you remain in charge throughout the altercation. Be aware of where the knife is at all times. For additional safety, tuck your chin and head down behind your shoulder.

4. The moment the adversary hits the ground, use the figure-four hold to force him to release the knife. Do not go down with him or release your grip on his arm. Use your legs or knees to press to any sensitive area of his body, preferably the head, to motivate him to release the weapon. If you can force him to his stomach through the figure-four hold or another joint lock technique, your positional superiority will increase.

Note that it is unlikely that an opponent attacking with the knife in the icepick grip will advance with the weapon in position for an overhead stab. He will likely pull the knife from his waistband or grab it from a counter or some other place, and advance while holding it low by his hip. This complicates your defense, because you will not be able to tell what type of attack is coming. Liken this to a kick in your empty-hand martial art. Most kicks start by raising the knee high, a position from which several kicks, including front, roundhouse, and side thrust can be thrown. When facing a skilled martial artist, you won't know which kick he will throw simply by observing the position of his knee. Likewise, when facing a skilled knife-wielder, you won't know what type of attack he will use, simply by the way he is holding the knife or by the position of his arm.

This is one of the simpler defenses against the icepick overhead stab. But success relies on that you see the attack coming. If the adversary draws the knife from his waistband and closes the distance just prior to raising the knife for the attack, defending against this type of stab will prove more difficult. Image source: TZAHAL, reproduced under Wikimedia Commons license.

Pressout defense against a slashing attack

When faced with an opponent wielding the knife in a forward or reverse grip slashing type attack, you must either distance yourself enough to make the blade miss or work inside of the attack. Martial arts instructors sometimes teach to step forward and block with the forearm to the inside of the attacker's arm (and we explored a possible defense doing just this in a previous section). But to succeed with this defense, we must assume that the arc of the knife is rather wide. If the attacker is proficient with the knife, he may engage in quick slashes close to his body and with his arm bent at the elbow, preventing you from moving inside of the attack without getting struck. If you can anticipate the attack, you might draw it with a sudden, unexpected move, gaining an opportunity to seize the initiative.

1. When the adversary attacks, step back and allow the attack to miss. Immediately step to the outside of the opponent's arm and pin the weapon arm against his body. Pinning above the elbow rather than below, gives you greater control by decreasing his mobility.

2. Press forward, forcing the attacker to retreat until he is off balance. Use your free hand to press against his jaw, simultaneously stepping behind him and tripping his leg to take him down.

This type of defense places you away from your opponent's centerline at a superior position toward his back. But your timing must be good, if you are to take full advantage of the missed attack. Once you decide to move in, stay as close as possible to stifle his movement.

Your opponent knows that the knife is a threat and is not expecting you to go after him empty-handed. When you take the offensive stand, you place him in a mentally inferior position.

Important: After the initial tie-up, you *must* stay with the technique. If you miss your opponent's arm or let your grip slip, use your shoulder to push him back. Remain at close range using techniques from your empty-hand martial art to take him down.

Defending successfully against a tight slashing attack with the knife in the reverse grip can prove difficult, because it requires extreme closeness to the blade and an ability to act with precision against the speed of the attack. If possible, attain the outside position and pin the knife arm against the attackers body, and then proceed immediately with a strike designed to hurt, or with a takedown. Image source: Martina Sprague.

ON THE GROUND

One of the dangers in a grappling scenario involving a knife is your extreme closeness to the adversary. When grappling with a knife-wielding opponent, even if you manage to pin and control his arm, as long as he has mobility in his wrist there is still a chance that he can cut you. He may only have enough mobility to do a surface slash to your forearm, for example, which will not take you out. Or he may have enough mobility to stab to a vital target such as your throat. Be aware of this danger even if you are skilled at ground combat. As an example, if your opponent holds the knife in the forward grip when you take him down, and you have achieved partial control of his arm while straddling him or while in the cross-body position, he may not have enough mobility to cut you. But if he switches to the reverse or icepick grip, he may be able to stab you in the neck.

Moreover, to successfully pin your opponent to the ground, you must be near his upper body or head. This also places you close to his arms and hands, and therefore close to the knife. Be prepared to protect your vital targets, particularly you neck.

Exercise: Sit on a chair and have your partner attack with the knife in the icepick grip. Your first concern is to avoid the stab. If you can't get to your feet and halt the attack, use a forearm block to avoid the first stab. Then get to your feet and drive forward to close the distance and seize the initiative, for example, by striking with a palm to the jaw. It is crucial that you hurt your opponent before trying to distance yourself from the encounter.

Remember that he still has control of the knife. Explore the possibility of using the chair on which you were sitting as a shield or weapon.

Exercise: Practice rolling with a partner on the ground. Have him wield the knife. Your only goal is to prevent him from cutting you. This means that you must prevent the blade of the knife from touching you. Explore ways to tie up your opponent's knife hand or hurt him enough to get a reaction that allows you to get away.

Exercise: Get down on the ground and have your partner attack you with the knife in the icepick grip from a standing position. When experimenting with this scenario, you might find that a strong kick to the kneecap might give you enough time to stall the attack for a few seconds. A solid kick to his jaw, if you can reach it, might also be a good defense. The question is whether it is enough to facilitate your escape. Try to get to your feet as quickly as possible. Rolling to your side to get to your hands and knees will expose your back, preventing you from using further offense while he is closing the distance. If you're on your back when your opponent approaches, he might also be able to grab your kicking leg and force your body on its side. You have now virtually no weapons available for further defense. Kicking your opponent might buy you a few seconds, but he will likely attempt a new attack.

Exercise: Examine the previous scenario from your opponent's viewpoint, too. If you are the one with the knife trying to attack a person on the ground, how would you get past his kicking legs? Is it better to cover up and approach slowly, or is it better to rush in and break through his defense? Can you take his kick on your arm, for example, and collapse his leg as he withdraws it? If this is possible, you might find that you can close the distance in no time, break through his defense, and attack almost unhindered with the knife. Remember your targets. You don't necessarily have to stab him in the heart or slit his throat. A kicking opponent will expose his leg and inside thigh area. If he is wearing low top shoes and you can catch his kick, you might be able to sever the Achilles tendon. You might also be able to stab the knife deep into the femoral artery on your opponent's inner thigh. See Book 4 of the *Knife Training Methods and Techniques for Martial Artists* series for a deeper discussion of targets.

Be aware that a deep stab to the femoral artery on the inner thigh can prove devastating. An opponent on the ground who is not in position to reach your heart, throat, or eyes might still be able to reach your thigh area with the knife. Image source: Martina Sprague.

If you are on your back on the ground and your opponent is straddling you with the knife in the icepick grip, your first concern is to avoid getting stabbed. Be particularly protective of your neck. If you are the smaller and weaker fighter, the only real option you have is to cause your opponent so much pain that his focus shifts from attacking with the knife to his own safety. The eyes are always vulnerable. Try redirecting the knife to the side of your head and immediately pressing your thumbs into your opponent's eyes. It should go without saying that you must exercise extreme caution in the training hall. Is this tactic possible if your opponent's arms are longer than yours, and he is holding you down with one hand while trying to stab with the other? Once you press your fingers into his eyes, it will prove easier to roll him off you. If you roll with him, you will end up in his guard (between his legs). Continue pressing your fingers or thumbs into his eyes while pinning his knife arm with your knee. If possible, pin below the elbow to eliminate the mobility in his arm.

If you reverse the previous scenario (you are now the knife-wielding attacker) and place yourself on top of your adversary, and he attempts to press his fingers into your eyes, make every effort to stab him with the knife before giving in to the pain. Chances are that at least one of several stabs will penetrate a good target such as the chest or heart. Be aware that if your opponent is wearing leather, such as a motorcycle outfit, it may prove tough to slash or stab through his clothing. You must now aim for a specific vulnerable target, such as his neck or eyes.

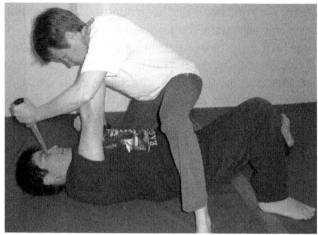

In a knife fight, the neck and eyes may be the most vulnerable targets. Remember that the knife gives your opponent reach. Trying to ward him or her off with a straight arm to the throat, as shown here, may not give you the distance you need to avoid the blade.
Image source: Martina Sprague.

Three ways to reverse positions on the ground

Let's say your assailant has taken you to the ground and is straddling you or is in your guard (between your legs) when he deploys the knife. You are in a very disadvantaged position, and meeting power with power will not work if you are the smaller or weaker person. You can achieve positional superiority by reversing positions.

If your opponent is in your guard and attempts to stab:

1. Wrap your legs around his body and grab his wrist

with both hands and guide the knife off your centerline and to the side of your head. This move does not require a great deal of strength. In principle it is almost like a parry where you redirect the force off the attack line. Liken it to deflecting a punch in empty-hand sparring.

2. Swing the leg that is on the same side as the opponent's knife hand around the front of his neck. If you have guided his right hand to either side of your head, swing your left leg around the front of his neck.

3. Use the strength in your leg combined with an arching of your back to unbalance your opponent to the rear. Maintain your grip on his wrist and apply a jujutsu arm bar as soon as you topple him backward.

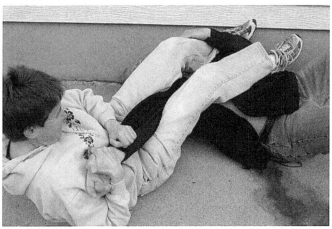

The jujutsu arm bar is one of the simpler and more effective techniques to learn when training for ground combat. Image source: Martina Sprague.

If your opponent is straddling you and attempts to stab:

1. Grab his wrist with one hand in an upward blocking motion to stop the attack. Guide the knife off your centerline and to the side of your head.

2. Simultaneously bring your free hand into play and apply a figure-four control hold the way you would if you were standing when your opponent attacked you with an overhead stab. Use the control hold to roll your opponent off you.

3. Use his higher center of gravity to pull you along until your positions have reversed and you end up on top. Pulling him close and keeping your center of gravity close to his (staying in close body contact) will assist you in using his momentum to your benefit. You will end up in his guard (between his legs), but you will be in a position of strength as long as you retain the figure-four control hold on his arm.

If your opponent is in the top position and attempts to stab, you can also:

1. Grab his wrist with one hand and guide the knife off the centerline and to the side of your head. This will bring his upper body forward.

2. With your other hand, grab his chin and twist his head to the side and back. This will start an unbalancing motion intended to roll him off you. Use his higher center of gravity to pull you along until your positions are reversed.

3. As soon as you achieve the top position, force his knife arm straight out from his body. Turn his head facing away from the knife and press with your free hand against his jaw to instill pain and convince him to drop the knife.

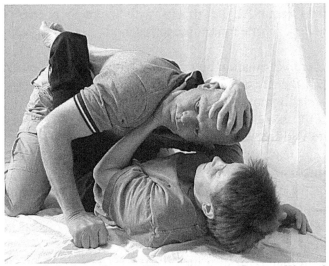

The neck is an inherently weak area. Controlling the adversary's head can help you control his whole body. One way to reverse positions on the ground is by pulling the opponent close, grabbing the top of his head with one hand and his chin with the other, and twisting his head to the side, using his momentum against him to reverse positions. Image source: Martina Sprague.

THE KNIFE AS A WEAPON OF COERCION

An adversary can attack with intent to kill, or he can attack with intent to coerce. If he attacks with intent to kill, you must respond immediately and fractions of seconds count. If he attacks with intent to coerce, you may have a little more time to respond.

A coercive situation could possibly escalate into intent to kill, if the stress level is high and the adversary interprets any small move you make as threatening. However, a benefit as a defender in a coercive situation is that the knife will likely be stationary and held where you can see it to increase its psychological effect. It may also be held against your throat. We have already talked about how a knife is most dangerous when in motion. A stationary knife, by contrast, gives you a decided advantage in that you know exactly where it is, which may present you with an opportunity to grab and control the knife hand, and ultimately disarm the adversary. A knife must touch you in order to do physical and not just psychological damage. If the weapon were a gun instead, it would make little sense for the adversary to get so close that you could grab it.

For defense, any object you find in the environment can prove useful for hurting your adversary or stealing his focus, and can include the obvious such as a gun, knife, or stick, but also the less obvious such as a belt, magazine, or a handful of sand. If the knife is not yet touching you, can you swing your belt at your opponent as a distraction? Can you remove some object from your pocket and throw at him, even if it is your wallet? You should ideally act before the knife touches your throat or other part of your body. This is true in empty-hand martial arts, too. When your opponent has established a good grip, it may be too late to execute a successful technique.

**Practice on a martial arts dummy to gain insight into different ways in which your adversary may control your head while simultaneously holding a knife to your throat. In a situation like this, any small move on your part may result in getting your throat cut, even if the opponent's intent is to coerce and not to kill.
Image source: Martina Sprague.**

Let's assume that your opponent points a knife at you while grabbing your throat with his free hand. Your natural reaction may be to grab the hand that grabs you, but this may not be your best option. By grabbing his hand or arm, you will also resist him at a point in his anatomy where his concerted focus and strength are at the moment. If you have mobility in your hands, you may want to try a straight punch, eye rake, or palm strike to his face instead. Any one of these strikes could hurt him, stun him, or move him back enough to give you the temporary strength advantage you need to defeat his hand on your throat. If you follow up immediately upon landing your strike, you may also succeed at taking his balance, disarming him, or continuing with some other attack that will neutralize the threat and allow you to escape.

If your opponent holds the knife to where it actually touches your throat or neck, by contrast, your primary concern is to get the knife away from you. The fact that it is a coercive situation may work to your advantage. A knife held stationary against your throat likely indicates that it is used as a threat and that your opponent wants something from you. His main concern is not to kill you.

As already discussed, rather than thinking in terms of specific techniques, think in terms of concepts, such as moving or knocking the knife away from your throat and immediately following with an incapacitating technique. If you knock the knife away, will your opponent have time to regroup and retaliate before you take him out? Experiment with a partner to find out what it takes. Please note that I'm not suggesting that any of this will be easy or safe. Even if your initial technique succeeds, you are still at risk of getting cut when the adversary reacts to your move. Note also that if your opponent is behind you when he presses the knife to your throat, you will have an entirely different set of circumstances to deal with. As you prepare your defense, remember that he will likely be very tense and may act on the threat and kill you, perhaps inadvertently, if he perceives a counter-threat.

In a coercive situation with your opponent behind you, even if the knife is touching your throat, it may be held loosely enough not to cut you. You may have been taught to grab your opponent's arm and pull it straight down, pressing it against your sternum as your initial defensive move. Experiment with a partner to determine how this technique will change the position of the knife and create an opportunity for escape. Although pulling the knife away from your throat may prove difficult, it may also enable you to throw your opponent forward over your shoulder. But your ability to succeed with this move relies on explosive speed and, naturally, some training in throws.

It is not obvious that a knife used as a weapon of coercion will be held against your throat. If your opponent holds the knife against your back instead, a quick turn of your body, with your arm deflecting your opponent's arm, can move the knife off the target long enough to allow you an opportunity to act with a greater offensive technique. But your initial move must be decisive and aimed at deflecting his arm. The moment you successfully deflect his arm, wrapping your arm around his at the elbow in an underhook can give you control, lock his arm, and place the knife past the boundary of your body. A good follow-up technique for rendering your opponent harmless might be an elbow strike to his head.

If you raise your hands high when threatened with a knife against your back, as seen here, you may decrease your chances of defending yourself successfully. Try to keep your arms as close to the level of the knife as possible. Image source: Martina Sprague.

When working on these techniques, keep in mind that a smart knife-wielding opponent knows the consequences of getting disarmed. He will ensure that your balance is slightly to the rear when placing the knife against your throat from behind, which will complicate your defense. He may also place the knife with the edge against the side of your throat, so that any slight turn of your head will result in a cut. When studying a defensive technique, always address what your opponent might do to negate it. Assuming that he knows more than you will keep you honest and illustrate that many defensive techniques, as learned in the training hall, will not work flawlessly.

Having a knife held against your throat is bad enough.

But having a knife held against your throat while simultaneously being forced off balance to the rear makes the situation exceptionally dire. Image source: Martina Sprague.

Furthermore, all fights that end with a knife attack don't start with a knife attack. As previously discussed, if his motive is to kill you, he will likely be fully committed to attacking with the knife, will do so in ambush, and will give you little opportunity to recognize the fact that you are in imminent danger. But if his motive is to convince you to give him your money or other material goods, or submit to rape or kidnapping, he will use the knife primarily as a threatening device. At the initial approach, he may have the knife hidden in his waistband. The encounter may therefore appear empty-handed at first, but may escalate to a weapon encounter later depending on his motives and whether or not you submit to his demands.

NEUTRALIZING THE THREAT

Now that you have practiced a few defensive moves, controlling techniques, and takedowns, let's talk more about what it takes to neutralize the threat. To neutralize the threat, think like this: Avoid the first cut. Then neutralize the threat by striking the eyes, throat, groin, nose, forehead, or other sensitive area, or by taking your opponent off balance.

Chances are that you will get some forewarning of the attack. For example, the situation may escalate from a verbal confrontation to a knife threat. You will have at least a small amount of time to absorb the warning signals and prepare yourself. But you might also be taken by surprise. If this is the case and the assailant is out to kill you, he will probably succeed. As emphasized by British soldier and hand-to-hand combat expert, William Ewart Fairbairn, there is no sure defense against an opponent armed with a knife. You can't do much if you have no idea that the attack is coming and it is executed with surprise, determination, and full intent. An opponent in a rage might rush toward you and execute several consecutive stabs to any part of your body within reach. Defending yourself against such an attack would prove exceptionally difficult. It is also possible that the assailant will take you by surprise, but does not intend to kill you. Once you have brought your initial shock under control, you can use previously learned martial arts techniques to neutralize the threat.

Keep in mind that when defending against a knife attack and disarming the adversary, you are not just defending against the weapon; you are ultimately defending against the person. When faced with an opponent who is angry, or crazy, or intent on hurting you, the greatest danger lies in him and not in the weapon. With this in mind, remember that a wimpy, sloppy, or inaccurate defensive move will not stop the adversary.

If you have access to a weapon, any weapon, it will strengthen your defense both physically and psychologically. Any object you can use as a shield to protect yourself or interfere with the movement of your opponent's knife is better than an empty-hand parry. A hard object such as a stick or a chair can cause significant pain if aimed at the opponent's hands. An adversary holding a knife is less likely to grab the stick or chair than is an empty-handed opponent, because holding a knife will deprive him of the mental focus or physical strength he needs to grab your shield with full expectation of success. This gives you an opportunity to use your shield as a striking weapon. Even a soft shield such as a jacket can be used to destroy your opponent's focus and field of vision, or to knock his knife hand to the side or down and force him to regroup. This is your opportunity to neutralize the threat. Don't give your opponent the opportunity to cut you. Remember that a knife encounter is not a duel. One cut may end the fight.

If using a stick to block or control your opponent's knife hand; for example, by striking the hand that is holding the knife, or by pressing the stick against his head or a joint in a ground fight, make sure you understand the amount of power required to redirect the path of the knife, halt the attack, or control the opponent. Striking the wrist or knife hand might be an effective option any time you have access to a stick or pipe or other hard object that also gives you significant reach. A forceful strike that fails to disarm the adversary may still do enough damage to split his focus. The moment he reacts to your blow, his primary concern is no longer attacking you with the knife. Rather than attempting to disarm him now, use your weapon to strike with full power to his head or other vital area such as his kneecap. When the damage is certain, you can distance yourself from the altercation even if he retains control of the knife. This example demonstrates how to neutralize the person rather than the weapon. When the person is neutralized, the weapon is also neutralized.

When you don't have the option to distance yourself from the encounter, speed and commitment are extremely important. Techniques can fail because of a number of factors. For example, you might lack the mental determination to fight a victorious battle and may therefore give your opponent too much time to evaluate and counter the attack. Remember that it ain't over until it's over. When the attack is inevitable, you must render your opponent harmless, whether this means disarming him, hurting him, or taking his balance. Whichever method you choose, your objective is always to ensure your safety. Neutralizing the threat should take no more than a few seconds. If it takes longer, you may lose your window for escape.

Exercise: Engage in some practice scenarios where your opponent starts the attack by punching or kicking and then pulling the knife. Next engage in some practice scenarios where your opponent starts the attack by grabbing or trapping your arms to control you and then pulling the knife. Finally engage in some practice scenarios where your opponent starts the attack by taking you to the ground and then pulling the knife. How would you respond in each case? In which scenario was it easiest to neutralize the threat? Your answer to this question may depend on your martial arts background. If you are a skilled karate fighter, you may have found your greatest strengths in the stand-up scenario; if you are a skilled hapkido fighter, you may have found your greatest strengths in the trapping scenario; and if you are a skilled grappler, you may have found your greatest strengths in the ground fighting scenario. There is a defense to every offense; there is a counter to every attack. The trick is learning how to use the empty-hand skills you have already developed when you are no longer fighting an empty-handed opponent.

Regardless of which type of martial art you have studied, a basic concept says that you can control the weapon and neutralize the threat by controlling the adversary. We tend to focus on the perceived threat: the knife, without focusing on the real danger: the adversary. You don't necessarily have to control the hand that is holding the knife in order to neutralize the threat. Image source: Martina Sprague.

ADDITIONAL THOUGHTS ON KNIFE DEFENSE DYNAMICS

Now that you have achieved some experience in dynamic knife defenses, let's talk about the philosophical aspects of the attack. At what point do you determine that you must defend yourself? If your opponent is advancing slowly with the knife, you will probably begin to back up and may try to talk your way out of the situation. But at what moment do you know with certainty that you must seize the initiative and counter the attack?

If you have retreated so far that you are standing with your back to a wall, it may be too late to defend yourself successfully. When you limit your mobility, you give up mental superiority. As a guideline, if you have to take more than three steps to the rear and your opponent is still advancing, it is time to seize the initiative and preempt the attack, providing that you have the knowledge and skill to do so, of course.

Exercise: Block off a twelve-by-twelve foot area (the size of a typical room in a house), and have your partner attempt to attack you with a training knife as fast as he can, stabbing or slashing as many times as he can in five seconds. Set a timer. This exercise will demonstrate that you will most certainly get cut no matter how skilled you are at blocking, redirecting, intercepting, or catching.

What you will discover when training in dynamic knife defenses is that applying a martial arts technique against a knife is extremely dangerous. Before taking action, and if time and circumstances permit, evaluate whether it really is the only way to save your life. Keeping the attack at bay while searching for an opportunity to get away without engaging your adversary may be the better option, if possible.

If calming the situation doesn't work, and the attack is imminent, a distraction aimed at your opponent might give you the time you need to thwart the attack. If you have access to a blunt weapon such as a club, maintain your distance from the adversary and strike his hands or elbows, or other bony parts of his body such as his knees or head if you can reach these targets without getting within range of the knife. The fact that you have a weapon allows you to seize the initiative by forcing your opponent into defensive mode.

If you throw an object at your adversary as a distraction, you must throw it with enough intent to achieve your objective. The object doesn't necessarily have to be heavy or sharp, but it helps if it does some damage in addition to distracting him. A fistful of sand thrown at your opponent might work, but a solid object, such as an iron pipe that you can swing with force and determination, might prove better. The distraction should ideally stop the adversary completely or hinder him in his pursuits long enough to give you time to get away. Swinging the object aggressively is more threatening than simply holding the object in your hand. Swinging the object aggressively also helps you prepare your mind and body for a possible physical engagement. Your actions should instill fear in your adversary. If they only anger him, you may place yourself in even greater danger.

Exercise: The greatest benefit of a weapon may be the

reach it gives you. To gain some insight into the mind of your knife-wielding adversary, place yourself in his shoes momentarily and imagine how you might feel when faced with an opponent swinging a stick or iron pipe wildly about him. You will probably feel fearful of closing the distance, even if you have a knife. You might even think of some way to end the confrontation gracefully without resorting to your weapon.

If you were holding a knife and the person you intended to attack had access to a stick that he or she started to swing with full force, you may not be so keen on using the knife but would be more concerned with your own safety. Image source: Martina Sprague.

If you can find no object in the environment to use as a distraction or weapon, and you must go empty-handed against the knife, where is the safest space where your opponent will have the greatest difficulty reaching you? If you can't run, can you take his balance by attacking his legs, for example, by ducking under the normal trajectory of the knife?

Exercise: Run at full speed and tackle your opponent's legs, using your momentum to get him to the ground. You can practice this on a Thai-style heavy bag at first. The attack must happen at full speed with no break in momentum to avoid giving your opponent an opportunity to brace himself or bend forward, stabbing the knife into your back. When you have practiced on the heavy bag, get with a partner. Determine the best time to tackle him. What distance lends itself best to the tackle? Should you attack him before he has made a move with the knife or after? Pad up as necessary and make sure you have a padded mat to fall on to avoid injury.

A leg tackle and takedown must be executed with speed and determination, in order to prevent the adversary from sidestepping the tackle or stabbing the knife into your back. Image source: Judcosta, reproduced under Wikimedia Commons license.

Exercise: A good weapon against a knife-wielding assailant is a chair. Grab the chair so that the legs are pointing toward him, preferably with one leg lined up with his groin and the other with his chest, throat, or face. Strike his wrists or forearms with the legs of the chair, moving it in a figure-eight pattern. Practice with a partner. Go lightly at first and use forearm pads and gloves to minimize the risk of injury to your hands or arms. You can also use the legs in a forward "stabbing" motion to force the adversary to retreat. Does he seem reluctant to close the distance and attack with the knife after he's been struck by the chair once or twice?

Why is the chair effective against a knife-wielding assailant, but not necessarily against an empty-handed assailant? While an empty-handed assailant can grab the legs of the chair and take it from you, a knife-wielding assailant is not likely to give up (or put away) his knife, because the knife gives him perceived strength. Yes, he might grab one leg of the chair with his free hand, but you can simultaneously twist the chair against the natural movement of his thumb and break the grip quite easily, particularly if you also move forward to force him to retreat.

Think about this: Because of adrenaline, a person engaged in an attack or self-defense situation may not know when he has been cut. The cut will therefore not cause the expected shock. If you get cut while in the process of protecting your life, you may not even notice that you have been cut until after it's over.

UNDERSTANDING PAIN

Understanding your reaction to pain, and knowing how you will react when taking a strike or getting a little banged up, is a crucial part of your self-defense training. How long does it take you to recover? What if the shock of the blow absorbs you mentally to the point that you can't continue? Giving up in a self-defense situation is not an option, and you should train with the mindset that it is not an option.

Since the risk of injury is so great when involved in a knife scenario, it's important to discuss and train in how to handle the fact that you might get injured. Even if an injury doesn't disable you physically, a cut will make you bleed. Bleeding will affect you mentally. It is also possible that you won't even know that you got cut until after it's over. If the injury is more severe, for example, if your hand is chopped off by a big knife, or if the knife is thrust deep into your abdomen and the attacker leaves, what can you do to get help or bring yourself to safety? How to handle injuries that bleed may or may not be discussed in your martial arts class. When a student gets a scratch in training, even if it is minor such as a nosebleed, is he allowed to go and get immediate assistance or must he first finish the activity he is currently involved in? When training for a real encounter, it may benefit you to continue sparring a while longer after incurring a minor injury.

It may also not be enough to tell an injured student to keep fighting. He or she might need some mental preparation before the incident to avoid getting distracted by the injury. If you get injured to the point that you can't use one of your weapons; for example, if you can't grip or punch with your hand, or if you can't walk because you have a broken leg, how can you continue defending yourself against a knife-wielding opponent? These are questions that should be asked. I'm not saying that your martial arts instructor should take injuries lightly or ignore treating them, but that these are issues worth exploring. At what point does your defense become meaningless? Or can you really accomplish more than what you think you are capable of? Try fighting barefoot on gravel when you're used to a soft carpet to simulate a leg injury or physical distraction.

Also ask how often it is possible to flee a scenario without getting involved in physical fighting? If you keep flight in mind as a viable alternative, you might find that running away is possible more often than not, whether prior to the encounter or once it's already under way, or even toward the end of the encounter. Never lose sight of this possibility.

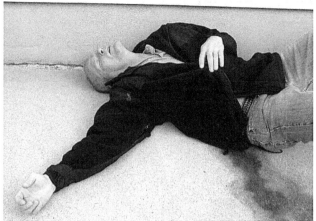

As a martial artist, how would you handle a situation where you have taken your opponent down and hurt him to unconsciousness, perhaps by banging his head against the concrete? Good martial arts training involves discussions about how to care for an adversary who is hurt, without increasing the risk of injury to yourself. Image source: Martina Sprague.

Knife-on-Knife and Multiple Opponent Knife Defense Strategies

Book 8

Knife Training Methods and Techniques for Martial Artists

by Martina Sprague

TABLE OF CONTENTS

Introduction	115
Brief History	117
Lesson Objectives	122
Multiple Opponent Warm-up Exercises	123
Three Multiple Opponent Knife Strategies	127
Thoughts to Ponder for Multiple Opponent Fights	133
Knife-on-Knife Basics	136
Martial Arts Dummy Practice	139
The Equalizing Power of the Knife and Other Weapons	143
Partner Practice and Knife Sparring	146
Knife Techniques Overview and Principal Concepts	151
Knife Techniques for Practice and Analysis	158

INTRODUCTION

Whether on the news or in action movies, most of us have probably seen footage of a helpless person lying on the ground, attempting to protect himself, while a mob is kicking him repeatedly to the body and head. Victims of these types of attacks generally sustain severe injuries, and there is little they can do once they end up on the ground. Although not totally impossible, it is also exceedingly difficult for a cornered person to run to safety past a mob intent on doing harm. While most of us probably have an opinion about what should be done in a multiple opponent attack scenario, I believe it is fair to say that most martial artists have never been in a situation that required them to fight several people at once, and certainly not with a bladed weapon. This leaves us at the theorizing stage, tempting us to promote common ideas, such as "line 'em up and fight one person at a time."

The intent of this book on knife-on-knife and multiple opponent knife defense strategies is to provoke you to think about and explore scenarios where you have a knife available but are facing multiple empty-handed opponents, and scenarios where you have a knife available and are facing a single opponent who is also armed with a knife, also called knife-on-knife scenarios. After practicing the techniques presented in this book, which may or may not work in these types of dangerous situations, you will find where the truth lies for you based on the training you have already acquired. Several techniques for practice and analysis are covered, which you can practice alone on a martial arts dummy or with a training partner, and which will assist you in building confidence, speed, efficiency, and timing. The techniques, attacks, and defenses offered in this book are meant for you to ponder; they are not meant to be definitive techniques on street fighting with a knife. Seldom if ever is there only one way to act and react in a knife encounter.

As explained in Book 1, the *Knife Training Methods and Techniques for Martial Artists* series has three objectives: The first few books focus on getting to know the knife, its strengths and weaknesses, and on manipulating and using it. The next few books focus on defending against knife attacks. The last few books focus on implementing empty-hand martial arts skills into your knife training, and include scenario-based exercises intended to bring your knowledge into perspective and give you a solid understanding of your strengths and weaknesses when faced with a knife-wielding assailant. Each book starts with an introduction. You are then given the lesson objectives, along with detailed information and a number of training exercises aimed at making you physically and emotionally ready to participate in traditional martial arts demonstrations involving a knife or, if fate will have it, in a real encounter. Remember that it is your responsibility to know and comply with all federal and local laws regarding the possession and carry of edged weapons.

BRIEF HISTORY

Regardless of which martial art you study, you will probably touch on the multiple opponent scenario sometime in your training. More often than not, however, we assume that the fight, whether empty-handed or armed, will take place against a single adversary. Forms practice might assume multiple attackers, but each imaginary opponent is still dealt with one at a time. Rather than defending against a group, you will in fact defend against individuals. When given the chance to participate in a multiple opponent attack scenario in the training hall, the semi-realistic way in which you practice will probably make you feel overwhelmed, as though the techniques you have studied so diligently have suddenly become useless.

To understand group dynamics, we must first understand how a group functions. When practicing in the training hall, we tend to put together a group of randomly chosen students, who have not discussed the objective of the attack with each other. Each individual will therefore attack singularly. But in order for a group attack to work the way it is intended, the members of the group must aim for the same objective. An effective group is therefore one in which the members have trained to function well together. An effective group is not any number of people randomly put together, but a gang of a few members who are highly in tune with each other. When facing such a group, it is particularly difficult to enact a successful defense with or without a weapon.

When engaged in a multiple opponent attack scenario, your objective is not necessarily to kill or knock every member of the group unconscious, while walking away unscathed. Deterring the attack or preventing it from escalating is more important than killing your adversaries. Remember that even if a group of people walk toward you in a threatening manner, each person in the group is not necessarily ready to engage you in a physical fight, particularly not when knives are involved. They know, as do you, that they can get seriously injured. Thus, the longer you wait before you act, the more time you give the group to attain a single-minded focus and decide whether or not they are ready to fight for their objective. If you allow them to take you to the ground, the situation is especially dire, even if they are unarmed and you have a knife. When they sense that you are helpless, their confidence will grow. It is unlikely that you can win when taking multiple kicks to the body and head.

Although you are a skilled martial artist and have trained repeatedly in a number of techniques, nothing may happen the way you have planned. Be ready to use all of your weapons, whether fists, feet, or knives. Your focus should be on motion to prevent your opponents from grabbing you and restricting the use of your weapons. Although attempting to talk your way out of a situation might prove successful, and talking may buy you time to size up your opponents and decide what to do, talking may also split your focus and give your adversaries an opportunity to close distance, surround you, and mentally prepare to take collective action against you.

From a defensive perspective, it is generally more productive to take rather than give ground. When you start training against multiple attackers, assume an aggressive mindset. Rather than attempting to avoid the attackers by running or circling them, take the initiative and attack he or she who is closest to you. Then attack the next closest opponent immediately. You have now become the attacker and they the defenders; the mental game has reversed. The same idea applies to a knife-on-knife scenario against one other fighter. Take the initiative and move forward with your attack to any target within reach. Yes, avoid his cut, but seek the initiative. The person who cuts first will likely have the upper hand, and the opponent will withdraw when he realizes he is cut. Training in multiple opponent attack and knife-on-knife scenarios will give you an understanding of the level of commitment needed to survive such an attack.

Fighting multiple opponents with a bladed weapon is not a concept specific to modern martial arts, and many of the commonly propagated methods for surviving a multiple opponent attack scenario may well have been drawn from historical sources. Seventeenth century Japanese swordsman Miyamoto Musashi emphasized in his famous treatise, *A Book of Five Rings*, that when necessary to fight one against many, you should draw two swords, one in each hand, and stretch your body for maximum reach, and then implement plenty of movement in all directions, until the attackers feel as though they are being chased in a single direction or into a corner that prevents their escape. Taking this suggestion to heart also means taking the initiative and attacking first, rather than waiting for the attack to come to you.

Musashi further suggested that you should aim your strikes at he who is the greatest aggressor, while cutting both left and right. To remain in charge, avoid pausing or halting your momentum. Ideally, Musashi said, you should "drive the enemy together, as if tying a line of fishes, and when they are seen to be piled up, cut them down strongly without giving them room to move." See Miyamoto Musashi, *A Book of Five Rings*, translated by Victor Harris (Woodstock, NY: The Overlook Press, 1974), 65.

Musashi advised us to avoid fixating so much on the sword (or in your case, the knife) that we forget about our other resources. Succeeding in a multiple opponent fight requires thorough practice. As can be deduced from Musashi's writings, the idea that we should line up our opponents and fight only one at a time is therefore neither new nor profound. The problem lies in how we implement this suggestion successfully in practice. Musashi was a master swordsman who had dedicated his life to training with the sword. But martial artists in today's world probably have other obligations to work, home, and family, and will not achieve Musashi's expertise. Although we can theorize about what should ideally be done when defending against multiple opponents, the scenario will likely not go down as planned. We may therefore have to deviate a bit from the traditional mindset and explore other options.

Miyamoto Musashi fighting multiple opponents, driving "the enemy together, as if tying a line of fishes, and when they are seen to be piled up, cut them down strongly without giving them room to move." Image source: Historia n°764 – Août 2010, page 45, reproduced under Wikimedia Commons license.

LESSON OBJECTIVES

Upon completion of this lesson, you should:

1. Have acquired insights into the difficulties of fighting multiple unarmed opponents with a knife

2. Have had an opportunity to practice precision stabs and slashes to the primary targets on the torso of a martial arts dummy

3. Have gained insights into the equalizing power of the knife and other weapons

4. Have developed an understanding of the value of knife sparring, despite the fact that most knife fights are not fought like duels

5. Have explored a multitude of knife techniques in part and in their entirety

6. Have experimented with knife variations suitable for your particular martial arts background and experiences

MULTIPLE OPPONENT WARM-UP EXERCISES

Advanced knife defense tactics include situations involving multiple attackers and knife-on-knife scenarios. We will begin with a discussion about multiple opponent attacks, the dangers you face also if you have a knife available, and how to prepare to defend yourself when a mob is closing in on you. Understand that the situations presented here are meant to trigger critical thinking; they are not meant to be definitive. Explore them with your martial arts buddies in the training hall. Question their validity. Taking your prior martial arts background into account, how might you change the techniques to make them work better for you?

Although the knife is your equalizer, don't forget about your other natural weapons, particularly your legs. Your legs are by nature designed for mobility. It should go without saying that when faced with multiple attackers, if you can run, this is by far the best defense. Somebody coming toward you asking for directions might want to distract you and open the way for a second attacker to emerge. This situation requires vigilance and can often be avoided altogether, by not stopping to engage in conversation or letting a stranger get near you. That said, the *Knife Training Methods and Techniques for Martial Artists* series is not so much about awareness as it is about training and understanding how to use the knife in offense and defense. The aim of the first part of this book on advanced knife defense tactics is to explore scenarios dealing with aggressive multiple opponent attacks, where engagement is crucial to your survival. Let's start with some warm-up exercises.

Preparatory Knife Defense Exercises Against Multiple Attackers

Your legs have longer reach than your arms, so you can generally reach an opponent with a kick before you can reach him or her with a punch or with a knife; although, the size of your blade will impact your reach. Initiating your defense with a kick can give you the time you need to deploy your knife. It can also give you the benefit of the initiative, as long as you throw the kick as a preemptive move to stun your opponent, hurt him, or make him think twice about attacking you, and not as a deterrent to keep him away.

1. Have two or three training partners close in on you from different angles. Have each carry a kicking shield so that you can throw your kicks with power without risking injuries. You will probably find it difficult to strike and kick with power nearly simultaneously in different directions, because the resultant force of your strike or kick will split. You cannot launch your momentum in more than one direction at a time. To strike effectively in two directions simultaneously, the distance to your opponents must be identical.

2. Focus on perceiving movement around you. Throwing powerful kicks when movement is involved, especially if your adversaries come from several directions including the rear, is a whole lot tougher than throwing kicks on a stationary target such as a heavy bag.

3. Your timing, power, and endurance must be superb to achieve optimal results. If you kick too soon, you will miss the target; if you kick too late, your kick will get

jammed. This exercise gives you insight into how a multiple opponent attack scenario can deteriorate until you are no longer able to defend yourself successfully.

4. Repeat the exercise, but after initiating with a kick, use footwork to close the distance and throw a strike. Your empty-hand strike will later be substituted for a knife. If one opponent is stationary and another is moving toward you, where is the biggest threat? Probably with he who is advancing. You may want to fight him first.

5. Place yourself in a corner where you are unable to escape. Have your training partners close in on you as a group. Your job is to muster enough aggression to get through this barrier and to safety. Rather than waiting until they are upon you, run toward the person nearest you, using the momentum of your full body to bump him aside or strike him. This exercise teaches you to become the aggressor and not the scared victim waiting to get attacked. Your single-minded focus should be to get out of the corner and through the barrier. Under no circumstance should you allow the attackers to push you back into the corner. For this exercise to succeed, you need quite a bit of momentum, which means that once you decide to act, you can't fall back and hesitate. Once you decide to act, there is no stopping.

6. When you have achieved some skill perceiving movement and defending yourself with kicks, apply these skills to knife fighting against multiple empty-handed opponents. The first concept is changing the angle continuously. We tend to think of an attack as coming toward us from the front. This is not necessarily the case. If you are a trained karate fighter, you will have certain

footwork and movement patterns that are particular to your art. Explore how you might use the knife in conjunction with footwork. Will you grip the knife in forward or reverse grip? I recommend starting with forward grip because of the extra reach it gives you, slashing at any target your opponent extends toward you, most likely his hands, while maintaining distance with your body.

A group of two or more aggressors suddenly turning toward you is quite intimidating, even if you carry a knife. Image source: Martina Sprague.

THREE MULTIPLE OPPONENT KNIFE STRATEGIES

We will now discuss some pros and cons when facing multiple opponents, and the strategies available to you. You are encouraged to explore these further in training.

Line Them Up

As Japanese swordsman Miyamoto Musashi emphasized four hundred years ago, the common suggestion today is still to line up your attackers so that you only have to fight one at a time, so that you are never sandwiched between two and never surrounded. Lining up your opponents, making them approach you from the same side, might also enable an escape route. By contrast, being sandwiched between two adversaries makes escape difficult. Once you add some realism to your training, you will probably find that fighting multiple opponents successfully is easier said than done.

Using the line them up and circle strategy and fighting only one person at a time, using him as a shield against the others, may prove possible if the situation has not yet progressed beyond the intimidation stage and has not yet escalated to physical contact. You may even find success talking your way out, using the closest offender as a pivot point to shield yourself against the others, who are waiting to see how the situation will unfold. For the purpose of your martial arts knife training, however, we will assume that escape is not an option, at least not initially, and you must defend yourself with the knife.

You must not only be quick on your feet and act before you're cornered, you must also have enough precision and power in your strike, kick, or knife technique to finish your first opponent with a single strike, or the others will quickly be upon you. If your opponents also carry knives, a single cut to a vulnerable target, such as your hand or wrist, may disarm you. If you're armed and they're not, they may be more reluctant to approach you, which is why the knife is an equalizer. But dispatching multiple attackers proves difficult even if they approach you unarmed.

The Group Attack

While the common advice is to line up the opponents and fight only one at a time, others point to that a street fight involving multiple attackers may not rely on a great deal of strategy and finesse; they will not wait their turn for the best time to attack, but will swarm you all at once. It will happen fast, so lining them up and fighting only one at a time is unrealistic. Explore your options if you're swarmed by a crowd of three or four attackers. If they swarm you, they are likely set on doing damage and not just intimidate.

As already discussed, for a group to prove effective, it must act with a single mind toward the achievement of the objective. Every person in the gang might not want to fight. Some might be present to give moral support to their leader; in other words, to intimidate you. If the fight is not preplanned, they might be reluctant to engage you, particularly if you are brandishing a knife. When the leader of the group engages you, the others might stand nearby in their "ready" stances, trying to appear intimidating, even if they have no intention to fight. Without proper group leadership, a multiple opponent fight may never materialize.

If the situation starts as a verbal argument, you will have more time to prepare a defense. Remember that a knife can only be used when within range. Deploying your knife before your opponents are within range may stave off a fight when they realize you have a weapon and they don't. Even if they, too, carry knives, they may decide that the risk of injury is too great. But deploying the knife prematurely may also give away your intentions by eliminating the element of surprise. If the situation escalates from a verbal confrontation, you might pretend to focus on what one attacker is saying, and use the element of surprise against the others by suddenly deploying your knife and stabbing he who is closest to you, and immediately moving out of range. This sudden defensive move may stun the person you were talking to and deter him from pursuing the fight.

If you fail to act with a sudden preemptive move and engage in verbal argumentation instead, you might increase the possibility of getting attacked by the whole gang. Seize the initiative and act when your opponent is not yet expecting you to act, when he (or she or they) is not yet quite ready to pursue an all-out fight against an edged weapon.

When Cornered

Getting cornered is probably the worst situation you can find yourself in. Martial artists tend to offer a lot of advice, but none is foolproof. So what are your choices? If you can't distance yourself, take the initiative and preempt the attack. I'm not suggesting that it is a good idea to pull a knife on another person simply because he appears intimidating. The assumption, however, is that the scenario has gone beyond mere intimidation, that you know that these guys are dangerous, and that you will get severely injured or risk death if you fail to act.

Unlike strikes and kicks, the knife is a touch weapon that can do significant damage with minimum power. You can strike in two different directions with speed, such as left and right or right and forward, without rotating your hips or body and without sacrificing the effectiveness of the technique. For example, you might preempt the attack with a quick slash to the opponent on your right, immediately followed by a quick slash to the opponent on your left. Even a wild swing, which may not prove effective in empty-hand combat, might prove effective with a knife. A series of wild slashes can cover a large part of your opponent's body and do more damage than a tighter technique. If you have the opportunity, go for any area where skin is exposed, such as the hands, arms, neck, or face.

If you carry a longer-type blade, your reach will prove significant. The moment your blade touches one of your opponent's extremities, he will withdraw his hand and likely be fearful of fighting you. It may also cause the others to back out of the fight, particularly if they are there for intimidation purposes. Holding the knife in the forward grip may benefit you because of the extra reach it gives you. While the reverse grip allows you to conceal the knife, you are not concerned with concealing it now. In fact, you want it visible as an intimidation factor, which may deter further aggression.

Seizing the initiative is important because it places you in the position of intimidator. Your opponents will naturally shy away when you swing at them wildly with an edged weapon. It may also open an escape path from a cornered position. As discussed in Book 4 of the *Knife Training Methods and Techniques for Martial Artists* series, a stab deep into an organ is generally more lethal than a slash across the body, but a slash can have significant shock value and halt further attack.

Who should you attack first? Probably he who attacks you first, he who enters your personal space, or he who you perceive as the greatest threat. If two people threaten you but haven't actually engaged you, when a third person appears on the scene with the intent to attack, you may start with him. If the other two are standing by your sides and you have not yet deployed your weapon, a quick eye rake or palm strike to the jaw might give you the space you need to deploy the knife and move forward to meet the third attacker.

Long blades give you a definite advantage whether fighting multiple empty-handed opponents or another knife-wielding opponent, as demonstrated by these Filipino soldiers using large bolo knives. Image source: DVIDSHUB, reproduced under Wikimedia Commons license.

THOUGHTS TO PONDER FOR MULTIPLE OPPONENT FIGHTS

When training with the knife in martial arts class, it's not assassination scenarios you're practicing. If somebody is set on killing you and has preplanned the attack, you will get very little if any warning and can probably not rely on the skills learned in class. Successful use of the knife in defense, or successful use of any martial arts technique in defense, relies on an awareness of danger before you're attacked. If the attackers' primary motive is not to kill you—they might want a material object, or they might want revenge by beating you up to teach you a lesson—your life may still be on the line, however, because the situation can easily escalate and death can come as a result of circumstance.

When practicing knife defenses against multiple attackers, you might start by reviewing the material in Book 2 of the *Knife Training Methods and Techniques for Martial Artists* series. If you have not yet deployed the knife as the assailants are coming toward you, they will sense danger when they see you reaching for it, and may speed up the attack or attempt to tie up your hands and foil your ability to deploy your weapon. Be aware that if someone walks toward you with his hands hidden in his pockets, inside his coat, or behind his back, he could be hiding a weapon.

A person walking toward you with his hands in his pockets may be hiding a weapon, or he may just want to ask for directions. Vigilance, but not paranoia, is recommended. Image source: Martina Sprague.

Concealing a weapon might hide the fact that you hold the superior position. But this assumes that you are a hundred percent committed to its use and not willing to try to avert a fight through intimidation tactics. You thus have the choice to deploy the knife while there is still distance between you and the assailants in the hope that they will back off when they know you are in possession of a bladed weapon, or leave the knife concealed and wait to deploy it until they are upon you. The second possibility depends on your commitment to use the knife when your opponents get within range.

As you initiate your defense, remember that the legs are good targets. If you limit your attacks to high targets, you risk getting your hands tied up (or cut if the assailants have knives, too). But if your initial defense is an attack against your opponent's foundation, with or without the knife; for example, a stab to his thigh or a sweep intended to take him down, you will split his focus from high to low, and your hands will still be free to pursue additional moves.

There will probably not be a lot of time for thought in a multiple opponent attack scenario. To create a threatening impression, multiple opponents may walk toward you side-by-side, or nearly so, steadily advancing, forcing you to retreat. Unless you're a fast runner on an open street, you will eventually come up against a barrier such as a wall or a fence, or you may trip over a curb of a fire hydrant or something else in your way, and have little choice but to fight. But your two arms and two legs will be no match for your opponents' combined eight or more arms and legs. Naturally, this places you at a distinct disadvantage, even if you are in possession of a bladed weapon.

So what's the answer? Which martial style is best suited for fighting multiple opponents in a knife fight? There is probably no easy answer to this question. You're always the underdog when facing multiple opponents, regardless of the extent of your training or whether or not you have a weapon available. If you can't avoid the situation, you must at least ensure that you have time to deploy your weapon before the group is upon you.

KNIFE-ON-KNIFE BASICS

Now that we have talked briefly about defense with the knife against multiple empty-handed opponents, the other part of advanced knife defense tactics involves scenarios where both you and your opponent are armed with a knife, or the so-called knife-on-knife scenarios.

How reasonable is it that you will be dueling with your opponent, or go knife-on-knife? An opponent armed with a knife, but who thinks you are empty-handed, gains confidence through the knowledge that the knife is a devastating weapon. But if you, too, pull out a knife, how he views the situation will quickly change. Even if you are physically weaker or of smaller build than him, he will sense a significant threat because the knife is a touch weapon that doesn't require strength or size to wield. Once he understands that the threat you are enacting toward him is equally severe as the threat he is enacting toward you, there is a chance that the threat will not develop into a physical engagement. Nobody with a desire to live will engage in a knife duel.

It is probably more likely that you will be taken by surprise by a knife-wielding assailant, than that he will engage you in a duel once you display your weapon. But for the sake of gaining insight into situations involving a knife against another person who is also armed with a knife, let's experiment with the duel scenario first.

Remember your targets. Unless the attacker deploys the knife from a concealed position and from very close range, he must extend his arm at least somewhat in order to reach you. A quick slash to his hand or fingers is a good way to start. If it doesn't render his hand useless, it will at least solicit a reaction that buys you time to attack a primary target that will end the fight. A secondary benefit is that a quick slash to his hand allows you to stay reasonably out of range of his blade, particularly if you're holding the knife in the forward grip.

If he is attacking in an inward slashing motion instead of a straight stab, another possible option is to stab into his armpit as your initial move. Your timing must be good and you must be prepared to move forward the moment he initiates his attack. For example, if he swings with his right arm toward your left side, block to the inside of his forearm with your free left arm, and jab the knife in your right hand into his armpit. This is a quick defensive move, where defense and offense happen almost simultaneously. The full defense should take no more than a second or two. A similar possible defense that ends the fight quickly involves blocking the attack with your free hand, simultaneously slashing across your opponent's neck.

While attacking the opponent's fingers or knife-wielding hand as your initial move ensures that he can no longer use his knife, you must also follow with an attack to a primary target designed to end the fight. The technique therefore requires a two-count to complete. By contrast, blocking his attack with your free hand allows you to go for a primary target right away with your weapon hand, and end the fight in a one-count.

Which is better? It depends on the situation, the type of attack your opponent uses, and in which hand he holds the weapon. If he swings inward with a right-handed attack, and you also are right-handed, you may not be able to go for his hand initially, because it would require a move with your knife hand across your centerline. You might therefore choose to block with your free hand and jab the knife into his armpit. If he swings inward with a left-handed attack, you can reach his hand, fingers, or wrist with the knife held in your right hand more easily. If he attacks with a straight stab from a low position, blocking the attack with your free hand may prove more difficult. The armpit may also not be exposed as a viable target; although, the throat might prove a good target.

MARTIAL ARTS DUMMY PRACTICE

Defending successfully against a knife in the midst of the chaos of an attack can prove difficult or even impossible, particularly if you limit yourself to memorizing long sequences of techniques or specific defenses to specific attacks. Technique sequences can prove valuable, because they create a base on which to build the rest of your knowledge. But this is not the same as saying that you must stay with a long sequence of moves in a real encounter. It's not important to follow the sequence exactly. What is important is that you get away unharmed or at least alive. A good martial art evolves over time. Or as has been said, the best technique is the one you can use when you need it.

At this stage in your training, you should be able to use the moves you have learned instantaneously and without thought. To achieve this objective, it is not necessary to learn a hundred defenses to a hundred possible attacks. Realize that there are only so many ways in which your adversary can hold a knife, and the specific grip he uses further limits the type of attack. This allows you to narrow your possible defensive choices and counterattacks to just a few.

There are essentially two ways to hold the knife: forward and reverse grip. Each grip allows for two possible types of attacks: thrusting and slashing. The rest is determined by the specific angle from which the attack is coming. It could be high, medium, or low; overhand or underhand; inward or outward. Although this seems like a lot of possible combinations, if you perceive the attack according to the clock principle, you will see that the area you need to defend is relatively small.

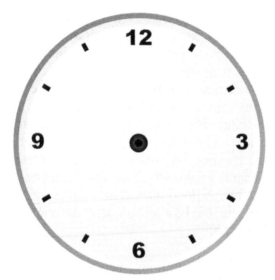

The clock principle is a good training device for learning directions and angles. Imagine each stab and slash directed at the eight major points, according to the face of a clock, in addition to one stab to the center. Nine basic stabs and eight basic slashes target just about every area on your opponent's body. Image source: Tkgd2007, reproduced under Wikimedia Commons license.

The same applies to you as the attacker. By using the clock principle in training, you will see that there are essentially nine basic stabs and eight basic slashes, which should all be directed toward the center to avoid overextension and wasted motion. What are these stabs and slashes? Imagine the face of a clock on your opponent's body. Draw a vertical line from top to bottom and a horizontal line from left to right. Now draw a diagonal line from upper left corner to lower right corner, and a diagonal line from upper right corner to lower left corner. You can now direct your stab into each of these eight lines toward the twelve, three, six, and nine o'clock positions for the vertical and horizontal lines, and toward the one-thirty, four-thirty, seven-thirty, and ten-thirty positions for the diagonal lines. You also have a straight stab to the center of the clock, which accounts for the ninth basic stab.

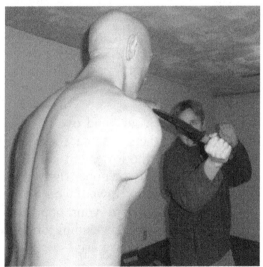

Practice combinations of the nine basic stabs and eight basic slashes on a martial arts dummy. Although wide motions are acceptable at first while learning target precision and instilling muscle memory, do not flail your arms. As you start getting comfortable, tighten the moves until no slash extends past the boundaries of the opponent's body. Protect your neck with your free hand throughout the exercise. Image source: Martina Sprague.

When gripping the knife, whether in forward or reverse grip, align the cutting edge with the first set of knuckles on your hand. Do not place your thumb on the butt (or pommel). All slashes with the knife in the forward grip can also be done with the knife in the reverse grip. The stab should be like a quick poke for speed, so that you can withdraw your hand in preparation for a new attack, and for protection against your opponent's counterattack.

When working stabs and slash combinations on a dummy using the clock principle, try a slash from the upper right corner to the lower left corner, for example, followed by a stab to soft tissue housing the organs; in this case, the liver. Explore each line, using both forward and reverse grip, on the face of the "clock," each time starting with a slash and ending with a stab.

Note that you must turn your hand over if slashing the opposite direction along the same line, for example, from the upper right corner to the lower left corner, and then from the lower left corner to the upper right corner. If the palm of your hand is facing toward you on the initial slash, it will be facing toward your opponent on the reverse slash, and vice versa, depending on if you hold the knife in the forward or reverse grip.

Remember, too, that human tissue is flexible. Learn to stab and slash straight and remain within the boundaries of your opponent's body. As in empty-hand martial arts, continuing a strike after it has passed the target results in wasted motion and may give your opponent an opportunity to trap your arm or to counterstrike. Protect your neck with your free hand.

THE EQUALIZING POWER OF THE KNIFE AND OTHER WEAPONS

Although the knife is an equalizer against a bigger, stronger, and unarmed opponent, when he also has a knife, the situation changes with an increased threat to your safety. If his blade is much longer than yours, you are at an additional disadvantage, and he knows it. A good exercise is to experiment with how different size and type weapons affect you psychologically. What if your opponent picks up a pipe when you come at him with a knife? At what point will his weapon halt your attack?

When training for offense or defense with the knife, include scenarios where your opponent has a knife, gun, club, or something else found in the environment. If he carries a pipe or stick, the impact can be severe. Make sure he misses with his first attempt to strike you. If he is determined to fight, he will attempt to strike you again. Since a stick has significant reach, he will hold the advantage unless you manage to get inside of the stick's effective striking range. The moment he misses with his initial attack is the time to close the distance, preferably by moving to a superior position toward his back. Remember that a stick is most powerful at the tip of the weapon. The closer you are to your opponent, the greater your chance of neutralizing the power in his attack. Jamming his attack and controlling the stick might allow you to control further movement and use your knife against him.

A good defense against a knife requires that you, too, are

armed. If your opponent is armed with a knife and you have access to an impact weapon, such as a stick, club, or brass knuckles, strive to block to his hand and not to his weapon. The block should be a striking block intended to do as much damage as possible. Your opponent cannot manipulate his knife without the use of his hands.

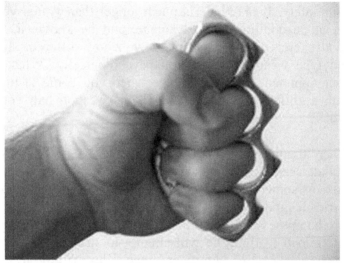

A set of brass knuckles or other impact weapon can prove an effective defensive tool against a knife attack, particularly if aimed at the adversary's hand. If you disable the hand that holds the knife, you disable further attack. Image source: Bahur, reproduced under Wikimedia Commons license.

Historical Gem: Carrying a saw-tooth knife comes with benefits and drawbacks. Historically, there were knives designed specifically for the purpose of catching an adversary's weapon in the teeth of the blade. Many such knives had only defensive capabilities, and a sword or longer knife was carried in the other hand for offense.

Significant wrist strength was also required to disarm an adversary if his knife wasn't caught just the right way. A straight spine that allowed the adversary's weapon to glide along the blade to the guard was often preferred over saw-teeth.

If using the knife to block your opponent's attack, use the part of the blade closest to the handle, or the strong part. Blocking with the tip or weak part of the blade may still place you in jeopardy of your opponent's blade, especially if he carries a large knife.

As you proceed with your training, remember that great power lies in knowing that you can, but won't. The greater your education on knife offense and defense, and on every detail that goes into a knife fight, the greater your confidence. An educated and intellectual person, and especially a martial artist, also practices self-restraint. This is a primary quality of traditional martial arts philosophy.

PARTNER PRACTICE AND KNIFE SPARRING

As discussed in Book 1 of the *Knife Training Methods and Techniques for Martial Artists* series, a true knife-on-knife fight is a rare occurrence, because both combatants know that their chances of surviving unscathed are slim. But training in the dueling scenario is still valuable, because of the instant insights it gives you into the frailty of life.

Despite the unlikelihood that you will duel with your adversary, knife sparring is a valuable training exercise that teaches timing that cannot be properly understood without sparring experience. Faulty confidence is often a result of the knowledge that practice knives are not sharp. Sparring sessions should therefore be limited to thirty seconds; you have only one chance to attack and defend. If you get cut, the engagement is over.

Start with designating an attacker and a defender to gain insight into how long it takes to receive a cut, when all you can do as the defender is block and move but not counterstrike or take the initiative. Now experiment with the dueling scenario, where you and your training partner are aggressors and defenders at the same time. Remember that there are few second chances with the knife. If you get cut, even once, you may go into shock or die. Multiple stabs in particular can prove lethal, but even a single cut to a primary target, such as the neck or midsection, can end a fight instantly. This is why knife fighting, even when practiced like a duel, can never be likened to an empty-handed sparring match.

You should now understand that you cannot afford to exchange blows with your adversary. In a boxing match, for instance, there are times when you are willing to take a blow in order to deliver one. This is not true in a knife fight. The idea is to cut your opponent while escaping unharmed. There is no such thing as "point sparring" in knife fighting. Although your fighting spirit may allow you to continue the fight and win even after taking a cut, the assumption that this is a viable strategy is dangerous. Therefore, you don't spar with knives, and you don't duel under a predetermined set of rules. You defend in one swift action that incapacitates your opponent. It's not only the right way, it's the only way.

So how do you start? If possible, avoid your opponent's first cut. Then move in immediately and countercut to a primary target, or counter from a distance to his knife hand. Although you seek the initiative and move to close range, acute awareness of his knife is crucial. Don't forget to use your natural weapons, your hands and feet, in addition to your knife. Use your free hand to protect your neck, block his attempt to cut you, or otherwise interfere with his movement and knife-wielding hand. A kick to your adversary's knee or groin might open an opportunity to move in with a stab to a primary target. It is preferable to trap or check the adversary's knife-wielding hand in order to immobilize it.

Engaging in a knife sparring session with practice knives teaches you that dueling is extremely dangerous. Attempt to stay out of reach of your opponent's blade, while swiftly attacking his knife hand to incapacitate him and prevent further attack. Image source: SuperMooh79, reproduced under Wikimedia Commons license.

Speed and determination are key. Holding the knife in your lead hand assists with reach and speed. Your mental composure, or your willingness to take the initiative, as has been discussed repeatedly, is extremely important. Although avoidance of the opponent's blade and defense against cuts is crucial, pressing the attack will generally benefit you, because it gives you the initiative and places your opponent on the defensive. Keeping your rear heel slightly off the ground aids with explosive footwork, which further increases your speed and unpredictability.

Do not engage your adversary or extend your knife hand without the use of good footwork in combination with the attack. Extending the hand while stationary exposes it as a target. Practice footwork, such as a step forward, back, or to the side, in combination with a slash or stab to your opponent's knife hand. It is naturally dangerous to come straight in against your opponent's blade. When stepping forward, even a small step to an angle will steal time from your adversary and place you in a more advantageous position, forcing him to adjust. This translates to time you can use to attack a primary target and end the fight. Proper use of footwork thus ensures that no time is wasted in the motion of your attack. Rather than stepping and cutting, which involves a two-count, cut within the motion of a step; thus, using only a one-count.

If your opponent is likewise pressing the attack and has remained a step ahead of you, or any other time you feel that you are not quite ready to attack, it might be necessary to disengage from the encounter by taking a step back. Withdrawing your lead foot first to place your lower limbs out of reach is preferred but, realizing that it is easier to theorize about life and death issues than apply these theories in the chaos of battle, any way you choose to step to get out of reach will do. Disengaging from the encounter doesn't mean that your mind goes into defensive mode. You still need to portray an attitude of offense by warding off your opponent's cuts, or by stabbing your knife toward his face to make him reluctant to close with you. If the stab strikes your opponent, then good. If not, it will at least place him on the defensive and give you time to back away and reassess the situation, and reengage from a stronger position.

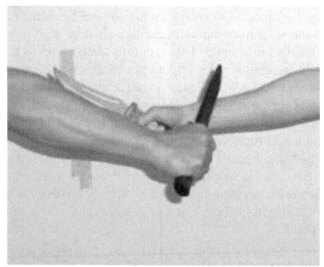

When going for the hand that holds the knife, use a quick cut to the knuckles or fingers. Do not attempt to reach the wrist as seen here. Taking the initiative and attacking first, as well as preserving distance is important in order to prevent a counterattack to your own wrist or hand. Image source: Martina Sprague.

KNIFE TECHNIQUES OVERVIEW
AND PRINCIPAL CONCEPTS

Technique practice done with precision helps you gain confidence in bladed weapon attacks and defenses. The knife attacks and defenses presented here focus on a series of techniques executed with dagger-type knives. Daggers have straight blades sharpened on both sides, tapering to a point. The most common type of dagger used in military combat may be the Fairbairn-Sykes version developed prior to World War II. The dagger is valuable since fine motor skills tend to deteriorate during an engagement. While single-edged knives, such as the Bowie, can be used successfully, it requires increased awareness of the direction of the cutting edge.

Historical Gem: Dagger-type fighting knives, such as the Fairbairn-Sykes and the U.S. Marine Raider Stiletto, weigh around a pound and a half and have the balance point near the hilt so that they stay secure in the wielder's hand. The Fairbairn-Sykes knife was manufactured strictly as a killing knife with a blade length of approximately six and a half to seven inches, and a grip nearly five inches long. Its light weight and long slender blade—British bayonet blades were used to provide "good quality steel for these knives"—was not intended for any other "utility" purpose. See Gordon Hughes, et al., *Knives of War: An International Guide to Military Fighting Knives from World War I to Present* (Boulder, CO: Paladin Press, 2006), 6, reproduced from *All-In Fighting* by Capt. W. E. Fairbairn and William A. Windrum, "Evolution of the F-S Knife," *Military Knives: A Reference Book*, from the pages of *Knife World*

Magazine (Knoxville, TN: Knife World Publications, 2001), 90.

The Fairbairn-Sykes knife is identified by its long and slender dagger-type blade and slim cylindrical, ribbed or checkered grip with a top nut. The design indicates that the knife was developed primarily for combat and not for utility purposes. Image source: Reproduced under Wikimedia Commons license.

The techniques presented here do NOT rely on "knife sparring" *per se*, but on three strategic phases designed to end the fight in the quickest way possible: managing the fight, killing the adversary, and securing safety against additional threats. Successful knife defense requires a strategy. The practitioner must understand the objective, be able to deploy the knife under pressure, and possess the mental readiness to use the knife against an adversary. Knife combat in general relies on only three techniques, with slight variations: the stab, the slash, and the block. The part of the blade closest to the hilt (the strong part, also called the *forte*) is used for defensive blocking maneuvers, and the part closest to the tip is used for attack and counterattack slashes. The stab should be executed like a quick and deep poke to a vital target. After penetrating the target, the knife can be withdrawn or left in place and twisted to facilitate a slash through soft tissue areas.

The techniques presented here represent the ideal way that combat might occur, and not combat in its "true" sense. It is thus important to recognize that various elements will be left to chance—or what early nineteenth century Prussian military theorist Carl von Clausewitz would have referred to as "friction"—and that the techniques may NOT ultimately work as intended or in their entirety. This is true for all types of martial arts practice, and should hopefully spark further debate that will broaden insights rather than diminish the value of the martial art.

All techniques presented here rely on basic moves designed to work in situations of great stress. It is assumed that you fight only one adversary at a time. If you choose to put the techniques together into a martial art form, it should NOT be viewed as defense against multiple opponents. The reason why you would use several directions and angles, and make the techniques flow without pause, is to preserve the historical context of martial art forms practiced in confined spaces that disallowed considerable movement.

How would you avoid a cut when your opponent is coming directly toward you? Do you have the space and timing to sidestep while simultaneously attacking his hand? If not, what other options would you try? Image source: Martina Sprague.

Before experimenting with the techniques, take some time to think about the following concepts:

1. Although a dagger is generally a weaker slashing weapon than a knife with a slightly curved cutting edge, it is assumed that the dagger edges have been sharpened for greatest effect. The techniques utilize both stabs and slashes. Stabs have historically proven more dangerous

than slashes and are therefore used to primary targets intended to end the fight.

2. Defenses focus on attacking the threat first; also called a secondary target, normally the adversary's weapon hand. This is done for the purpose of controlling the fight, disarming the opponent, or stalling the attack by forcing him to withdraw his hand.

3. A primary target designed to end the fight is attacked next. The primary target is normally located on the neck or upper body and can include a large blood vessel, the heart, or another vital organ such as the kidneys, liver, stomach, or intestines.

4. Finally, a target intended to take the adversary's mobility and ensure victory is attacked, generally the tendons by the knee.

5. As the adversary's mobility is taken, simultaneously assume an angle approximately 45-90 degrees from the original line of attack, and preferably toward your opponent's back. This is done in order to ensure safety, cause the opponent to readjust his position (in the unlikely event he is still standing), and allow you to flee additional threats.

6. Kicks are used to establish appropriate distance and gain time to counterattack. Kicks are used sparingly, however, and are not the focus of the techniques.

7. Small adjustment steps are taken throughout the techniques to compensate for various distances and

angles. The free hand guards the neck primarily, or other vital targets as necessary throughout the engagement.

8. Good targets are generally any soft tissue areas that are not protected by bone, including the torso, limbs, and armpit.

Although the techniques involve switching from forward to reverse grip and vice versa a number of times, it is not recommended that you do so in the middle of an engagement because of the risk of losing the knife and the time it takes to switch grip. Think instead of a technique as if it were composed of only two or three moves at the most. Thus, what is presented as one technique, involving perhaps five or six individual strikes, can now be broken down into two or even three separate techniques, each involving only two or even one strike. The idea is to end the fight as quickly as possible. That said, practicing how to switch grip helps familiarize you with your weapon and gives you confidence in its handling characteristics.

How you fight with a knife, and the particular defenses you choose against an opponent armed with a knife, will be based on your background, how you have trained, and the types of martial arts you have studied. When you have practiced and analyzed the techniques, design your own knife techniques based on your particular style of martial art, and practice them with realistic timing and execution. Work from both inside and outside positions in relation to your opponent. Work with your training partner empty-handed or armed with a knife. Work with him wielding a knife in the hand that is not normally the primary attack hand.

If you take your opponent down by disarming him and taking his foundation, pursuing the fight on the ground, as seen here, is not recommended, even if you hold the advantage through the knife. There is always a chance that fortunes will turn. Image source: Martina Sprague.

KNIFE TECHNIQUES FOR PRACTICE AND ANALYSIS

The knife techniques presented here are performed with one dagger in the right hand, or with two daggers, one in each hand. If you are left-handed, you can naturally grip your knife with the left hand and make other appropriate adaptations.

The first eight techniques call for defense using a single knife; the last six techniques call for defense using two knives. The grip is switched from the forward grip (also called fencing grip) to the reverse grip (also called icepick grip) as needed to facilitate speed, reach, and angle. When you have practiced the techniques with double-edged daggers, practice with single-edged knives, and decide what types of changes are needed due to the single cutting edge.

It is not necessary to learn the techniques in their entirety and exactly as they are written. Rather, choose parts of a technique and analyze its strengths and weaknesses. If a technique calls for switching from forward to reverse grip, or vice versa, could you have performed the technique successfully also without switching grip? If a technique calls for several moves, could you have combined defense and offense into just a few moves, or even a single move? Choose any segment of a technique for partner practice and analysis. Martial arts are meant to be fluid and instill muscle memory without instilling rigidity. When you have practiced the techniques as suggested, have your partner attack with the other hand; for example, if the technique calls for a defense against a right strike or knife attack, have him attack with a left strike or knife attack.

Note that "left" and "right," when discussing strikes to the opponent's body, is from his perspective. For example, a slash to the left side of his neck means *his left*, not your left.

Before proceeding, let me reiterate that the following information is for martial arts training purposes only, in order to gain a greater understanding of the power of bladed weapons and the brevity of human life. The author does not endorse the use of edged weapons as a means for resolving conflict. The instruction presented here and in other books of the *Knife Training Methods and Techniques for Martial Arts* series is purely informational in purpose and intended to strengthen the martial artist's empty-hand skills.

Technique 1: Defense against a right front kick or knee strike to the groin or midsection, or against a straight stab to the midsection.

1. Hold the knife in the reverse grip concealed behind your right forearm. Step into a right stance as you switch to forward grip and drive the cutting edge into the opponent's shin, upper thigh, or wrist depending on the type of attack he uses. Reinforce the defensive move with your free hand by applying pressure against the hilt. Since the dagger has two sharp edges, apply pressure against the hilt and not directly against the blade.

2. Slash diagonally upward to the front of opponent's throat. Follow with a downward diagonal stab to the left side of his neck. A variation is to combine steps 1 and 2 and, instead of a reinforced block to the wrist, slash the wrist and immediately follow with a slash to the throat. You can also step forward to the inside of the attack, block with your forearm and simultaneously slash to the throat.

3. Take a small step to your left, as you twist the knife with the palm of your hand facing toward you, and slash downward through opponent's neck. Follow with an upward diagonal stab to the right side of his body (liver).

4. Switch to reverse grip and slash diagonally downward to the left and right sides of opponent's neck. Then stab through or between the collar bones and into the heart.

5. If the knife is sharp and strong (as assumed), pull it straight toward you while using your free hand as a check in the opposite direction. You can also reverse the direction of the stab prior to pulling the knife toward you and stepping back to a left stance.

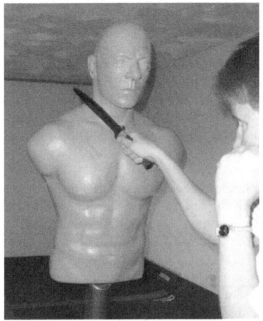

A quick slash to the side of the neck or throat is a good move after you have defended against the initial attack and disabled your opponent's hand. Image source: Martina Sprague.

Technique 2: Defense against a left punch, or against an attack with a knife or other weapon in a roundhouse-type fashion.

1. From a left stance, hold the knife in reverse grip and block with the cutting edge to the inside wrist or forearm to neutralize the threat and disable the opponent's knife hand. A slightly flexible wrist will aid the slashing ability of the knife. Execute a quick slap with your free hand to opponent's forearm near the

wrist to facilitate the disarm. Bring your free hand back to the guard position.

2. Drive the knife toward the opponent's throat, palm down, as if throwing a straight horizontal punch. Turn your hand palm up and reverse the motion, pulling the knife toward you while slashing the right side of his neck. Use your free hand as a check in opposing motion.

3. Stab to the left side of opponent's neck, then step to the rear with the left foot and stab upward to the right side of the abdomen, by dropping your hand low and angling your elbow slightly up and toward your opponent.

4. With the knife in reverse grip, slash toward the right of opponent's body through the liver, simultaneously stepping forward to the outside superior position with your left foot.

5. Angle out (turn clockwise) and slash the tendons at the back of opponent's right knee.

The abdomen or any organ in the midsection can be reached with an upward stab with the knife in reverse grip from close range, by dropping your hand low and angling your elbow slightly up and toward your opponent. Image source: Martina Sprague.

Technique 3: Defense against an opponent approaching from the rear in a threatening manner with a knife in the left hand.

1. Throw a right side or back kick to opponent's abdomen to halt his advance and gain the space and time needed to deploy your knife and ready it for defense. The opponent will likely react to the kick by reaching his hands forward.

2. Deploy your knife in the forward grip for reach. Close distance by shuffling forward from a right stance. Slash the top of opponent's left hand in an outward motion. Then slash his left hand in an inward motion.

3. Close the distance even more by sidestepping to your right, simultaneously slashing from left to right across the left side of opponent's body.

4. From a position to the side and slightly to the back of opponent, stab into his left kidney.

5. Angle out (turn counterclockwise) and slash the tendons at the back of opponent's left knee.

Technique 4: Defense against a right punch, or against an attack with a knife or other weapon in a roundhouse-type fashion.

1. From a right stance with the knife in forward grip, block the attack to the inside wrist of opponent's right arm. Follow with a stab to the right side of his neck.

2. Step back into a left stance to neutralize space limitations, while twisting the knife with your palm down and slashing through the throat. Follow with a slash to the biceps and inside of opponent's left arm and down to his hand.

3. Stab upward to the midsection, pull the knife toward you and switch to reverse grip.

4. Slash the tendons at the inside of opponent's right knee, then angle out (turn clockwise) and slash the tendons at the back of the right knee.

5. Finish with a left sidekick to the kneecap.

Technique 5: Defense against an opponent approaching from the rear in a threatening manner with the right leg forward and a knife in the left hand.

1. From a right stance and with the knife in reverse grip, slash to opponent's right wrist.

2. Slash diagonally downward to the left and right sides of opponent's neck. Follow with a stab through or between the collar bones and into the heart.

3. Drop your hand low and angle your elbow slightly up and toward your opponent, and stab upward to the groin or midsection.

4. Slash the femoral blood vessels in opponent's right leg, or the tendons at the back of his left knee if this leg is more conveniently located.

5. As the opponent goes down, finish with a left spinning back kick to his midsection or head.

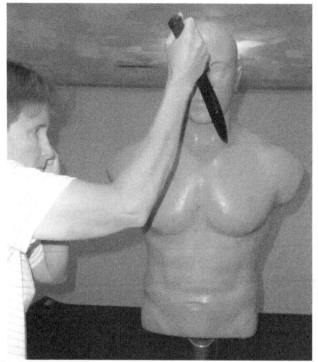

The heart is a vital organ. You may be able to reach it by stabbing downward through or between the collar bones. Image source: Martina Sprague.

<u>**Technique 6:**</u> Defense against a right knee strike.

1. From a right stance with the knife in reverse grip, execute a right forearm block to opponent's thigh, cutting the thigh simultaneously.

2. Slash diagonally upward and to your right across opponent's body and throat. Follow with a stab to the left side his neck.

3. Drop your hand low and angle your elbow slightly up and toward your opponent, and stab upward to the groin or midsection.

4. Switch to forward grip and stab upward to the throat.

5. Finish with a right front kick to the chest or chin.

Technique 7: Defense against a right roundhouse kick.

1. From a right stance, block the kick with your free arm, using an outward forearm block. With the knife in the forward grip, simultaneously stab to the inner thigh, puncturing the femoral blood vessels.

2. Slash diagonally upward and to your right, across opponent's body and throat. Follow with a stab to the left side of his neck.

3. Pull the knife out, or twist it and slash through the opponent's throat and diagonally downward across his abdomen. Follow with a stab to the liver.

4. Twist the knife and slash horizontally and to the right across opponent's abdomen. Follow with stab to the left kidney.

5. Angle out (turn counterclockwise) and slash the tendons at the back of opponent's left knee.

Technique 8: Defense against a right punch, or against an attack with a knife or other weapon in a roundhouse-type fashion.

1. From a right stance with the knife in reverse grip, block to the inside wrist of opponent's right arm.

2. Check with your free hand to the inside forearm of opponent's right arm, simultaneously slashing the triceps of his right arm.

3. Hook the knife over the top of opponent's right arm and pull toward you, while trapping his wrist in the crook of your left arm.

4. Drive the knife horizontally toward opponent's throat, palm down as if throwing a straight horizontal punch. Turn your hand palm up and reverse the motion, pulling the knife toward you while slashing the right side of his neck.

5. Step back to a left stance and throw a left sidekick to opponent's midsection or ribs.

Technique 9: Defense against a right overhand strike with a knife or other weapon in the right hand.

1. With one knife in your right hand in forward grip, pull a second knife with your left hand in forward grip from the back of your belt. For easiest deployment, the knife should be positioned vertically in your belt with the handle angled slightly to your left.

2. From a left stance and with both knives in forward grip, step slightly to the left and block the strike with an X-block to the outside of opponent's forearm and wrist.

3. Slash with the left knife along the arm and toward opponent's armpit; slash with the right knife in the opposite direction toward his wrist.

4. Stab upward with the right knife to opponent's abdomen; slash inward with the left knife across soft tissue areas on the right side of his torso.

5. Switch the right knife to reverse grip and slash vertically upward through the groin area.

Technique 10: Defense against an opponent approaching in a threatening manner with or without a weapon.

1. With the knife in your right hand in reverse grip and the knife in your left hand in forward grip, step with your right foot toward the approaching adversary and stab with the knife in your right hand straight to his throat to neutralize the threat.

2. Twist the knife in your right hand, palm up, and slash outward through opponent's neck. Follow with a slash with the knife in your left hand, palm up, across the right side of opponent's neck.

3. Reverse the direction of both hands and slash with the knife in your left hand, palm down, across the left

side of opponent's neck, and with the knife in your right hand, palm down, across the abdomen.

4. Finish with a right front kick to opponent's body or head.

Technique 11: Defense against an opponent approaching in a threatening manner, reaching out with both hands as if attempting to grab you.

1. Throw a right sidekick to opponent's ribs or abdomen to halt his advance and gain the space and time needed to deploy the knives and ready them for defense.

2. From a right stance with both knives in the forward grip, block to the insides of opponent's outstretched forearms (knife in your right hand blocks to his left arm; knife in your left hand blocks to his right arm).

3. Slash inward with the knife in your right hand to the left side of opponent's neck, simultaneously slashing inward with the knife in your left hand to the right side of opponent's neck, palms up, in an X-pattern.

4. Slash outward with the knife in your right hand to the right side of opponent's neck, simultaneously slashing outward with the knife in your left hand to the left side of opponent's neck, palms down, in an X-pattern.

5. Stab with both knives upward into the liver and spleen respectively.

6. Switch both knives to reverse grip and slash with the knife in your right hand across opponent's midsection, followed by a stab to the liver. Slash with the knife in your left hand across opponent's midsection, followed by a stab to the stomach.

7. Angle out (turn counterclockwise) and slash the tendons at the back of opponent's left knee with the knife in your right hand.

Technique 12: Defense against a right punch, or against an attack with a knife or other weapon in a roundhouse-type fashion.

1. From a left stance with both knives in reverse grip, block with the knife in your left hand to the inside of opponent's right wrist or forearm.

2. Slash with the knife in your right hand to the triceps of opponent's right arm. Follow with a slash across his throat, palm up.

3. Slash with the knife in your left hand to the right side of opponent's neck, palm down. Follow with a right knee strike straight up to his groin.

4. When opponent bends forward, stab with the knife in your right hand to the back of his neck.

Technique 13: Defense against an opponent approaching from the rear in a threatening manner with or without a weapon.

1. Throw a right back kick to opponent's midsection or chest to halt his advance and gain the space and time needed to deploy the knives and ready them for defense.

2. From a right stance switch the knife in your right hand to forward grip for reach, slash the left side of opponent's neck.

3. Step forward and slightly to the right and slash with the knife in the your left hand and reverse grip across opponent's throat.

4. Continue stepping behind opponent, while hooking the knife in your left hand around the back and to the right side of his neck.

5. Slash to the right side of opponent's neck with the knife in your right hand, palm down. Follow with a stab to the right kidney with the knife in your right hand, and a slash to the left kidney with the knife in your left hand.

6. Angle out (turn counterclockwise and slash the tendons at the back or side of opponent's right knee with the knife in your right hand.

7. As opponent goes down, switch the knife in your right hand to reverse grip, and stab downward with both knives into the back of opponent's neck and spine (or choose other targets as appropriate depending on how he falls).

Knife Training Methods and Techniques for Martial Artists

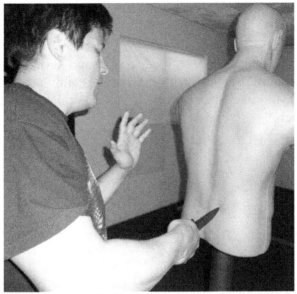

The kidneys are vital organs. A stab to the kidney if you manage to get behind your opponent, would likely end the fight. Image source: Martina Sprague.

Technique 14: Defense against an opponent approaching with the intent of coming to the aid of his fallen comrade.

1. With both knives in the forward grip, drive the edges of both knives in an X-block motion into opponent's throat.

2. Slash diagonally downward and outward with both knives simultaneously to the blood vessels on both sides of opponent's neck.

3. Stab with both knives diagonally upward to the liver and stomach.

4. Switch both knives to reverse grip and slash inward across the midsection, with both knives simultaneously in an X-motion. Stab with both knives straight into the abdomen.

Knife and Empty-Hand Defenses Compared

Book 9

Knife Training Methods and Techniques for Martial Artists

by Martina Sprague

TABLE OF CONTENTS

Introduction	177
Brief History	182
Lesson Objectives	186
A Few Pointers Prior to Technique Practice	187
Empty-Hand and Knife Comparisons in Stance Practice	199
Empty-Hand and Knife Comparisons in Blocking Practice	217
Empty-Hand and Knife Comparisons in Target Practice	227
Empty-Hand and Knife Comparisons in Striking and Kicking Practice	233
Empty-Hand and Knife Comparisons in Grab Technique Defenses	244
Empty-Hand and Knife Comparisons in Punch Technique Defenses	257
Empty-Hand and Knife Comparisons in Forms Practice	266

INTRODUCTION

Now that you have armed yourself with considerable knowledge about knife offensive and defensive techniques and concepts through the previous books in the *Knife Training Methods and Techniques for Martial Artists* series, you will start using the knife to enhance the techniques you already know from your empty-hand martial art. By practicing the exercises in this book, you will understand how your empty-hand skills can be used the way you have learned also when armed with a knife. You will learn that most empty-hand and knife techniques are interchangeable, or nearly so, with only minor adjustments. The knife can thus be used as an enhancement tool to build speed and precision in your empty-hand techniques. Moreover, should you find yourself in a self-defense situation where you have access to a knife, the muscle memory you have developed by practicing the techniques in your empty-hand martial art will be easily transferable to a large arsenal of knife techniques.

The knife is a simple weapon that is dangerous also in the hands of an untrained person. Knives are widely available in every home. Also knives not specifically designed for fighting, such as kitchen knives, can be used in defense against an attacker. It takes little or no training to injure, maim, or kill with the knife. If you have access to a knife and your adversary is unarmed, as long as you are mentally prepared to use the knife, you clearly have the upper hand, even if you have never studied a martial art. Gaining proficiency in an empty-hand martial art, by contrast, requires years of dedicated practice. You must learn many specific techniques and movement patterns, often in addition to kata (forms) and free sparring. So, if the knife is such a simple weapon, and an empty-hand martial art is such a sophisticated activity, won't it seem unfair to practice knife techniques against an unarmed training partner, as is the focus of this book?

It has often been said that the knife (or any weapon) is merely an extension of your hand. But this is not entirely true. Although you can use the knife in your empty-hand martial art in accord with the techniques you already know, as we will explore in this book, some adjustments are necessary when you transition from empty-hand to knife. For example, while hip or body rotation is often crucial for power in your empty-hand martial art, due to the knife being a touch weapon that can do damage using an insignificant amount of power, hip and body rotation prove less important when wielding a knife and may even slow you down or otherwise interfere with your knife techniques. In some instances, focusing on hip and body rotation when armed with a knife can potentially harm your ability to seize the initiative (to be first) and attack your opponent before he attacks you. The full lunge and rotation of your body, as in a sport fencer's thrust, for example, will take too long when armed with a knife, and could also jeopardize your ability to move to safety quickly.

Although the forward grip is frequently called a fencing grip, a wide sport fencer type lunge and thrust, as demonstrated here, is not needed for the achievement of penetrating power and could jeopardize your ability to reset your stance, cover your openings, and prepare for another attack. Image source: Martina Sprague.

The forward grip is sometimes called a fencing grip, because the knife is held the way a sport fencer holds his or her fencing foil. You might have noticed how a sport fencer extends the weapon through the lunge and by extending the arm entirely toward the opponent. As long as he acts before his opponent does, this may allow him to score a point also from considerable distance without placing himself within reach of his opponent's weapon. This tactic is rarely practical in a knife fight, however, which is not a sport in the same sense as fencing is a sport.

Going knife against knife, as explored in Book 8 of the *Knife Training Methods and Techniques for Martial Artists* series, may also require a different range than when both you and your opponent are empty-handed. Timing is crucial both in empty-hand and weapon practice, but, because of the dangers of the knife, perhaps more so when facing a weapon-wielding adversary. That said, implementing the knife into already learned empty-hand martial arts techniques will help you enhance those techniques and gain further familiarity with the knife as a martial arts weapon. It will show you how and when you must alter a technique in order to remain effective with the weapon, while still remaining within the basic framework of the original technique.

As you proceed with the exercises in this book, remember that it is not your opponent or practice partner who has a knife; he or she is empty-handed. You have the knife and are using it against his empty-hand strike or grab attempt. This may differ from what you typically find in other martial arts knife training books, which tend to emphasize empty-hand defenses against knife attacks. Although this book takes the opposite approach by teaching you to defend with the knife against an empty-hand attack, which may seem like a huge advantage in your favor, the purpose is to enhance your skill as a martial artist by relying on already acquired muscle memory, and learn to discern movement patterns that work whether you are empty-handed or armed with a knife. The techniques herein should therefore be viewed primarily in light of a training and not street fighting setting.

As explained in Book 1, the *Knife Training Methods and Techniques for Martial Artists* series has three objectives: The first few books focus on getting to know the knife, its strengths and weaknesses, and on manipulating and using it. The next few books focus on defending against knife attacks. The last few books focus on implementing empty-hand martial arts skills into your knife training, and include scenario-based exercises intended to bring your knowledge into perspective and give you a solid understanding of your strengths and weaknesses when faced with a knife-wielding assailant. Each book starts with an introduction. You are then given the lesson objectives, along with detailed information and a number of training exercises aimed at making you physically and emotionally ready to participate in traditional martial arts demonstrations involving a knife or, if fate will have it, in a real encounter. Remember that it is your responsibility to know and comply with all federal and local laws regarding the possession and carry of edged weapons.

BRIEF HISTORY

Although a small folder or pocket size knife is easy to carry on your person, a longer blade proves more effective for defending against an empty-hand or armed attack. When practicing knife techniques within the confines of your empty-hand martial art, it is recommended that you use a practice knife with a blade measuring at least six inches to get an accurate indication of how to use the knife to enhance your empty-hand techniques. You want a knife that is sturdy enough to block an incoming attack, that reaches your target with accuracy, and that allows you to use the pommel for striking. Most common martial arts practice knives meet these requirements. It is also important that the knife feels comfortable in your hand. If you have small hands, a large or thick handle may not be your best choice.

If you're going to carry a knife for self-defense, you must be prepared to use it if need be. However, even if you don't intend to carry a knife, practicing with one in the martial arts brings you several benefits. It will enhance your hand speed and precision also when reverting to empty-hand techniques; it will teach you about movement and positioning; and it will enhance your ability to seize the initiative in a confrontation, particularly if your adversary is also armed.

When training with the knife for the purpose of enhancing your empty-hand martial arts techniques, a sheath for carrying the practice knife is not necessary. Secure the knife in your belt when not in use, or simply forego the act of deploying the knife and start with it already in your hand. If you choose to secure it in your belt, think about how to carry it to facility a draw with your dominant hand (your right hand if you are right-handed). Some carrying positions are neutral; for example, vertical carry with the handle facing upward along the centerline of your body. This position facilitates a draw with either hand. For the purpose of the following exercises, however, most of your knife techniques will be done with your dominant hand.

The vertical carry position along your centerline facilitates a draw with either hand. Be aware of which direction the cutting edge is facing. If carrying a single-edged knife, the cutting edge should be facing down when drawing the knife in forward grip, and toward your forearm when drawing the knife in reverse grip. Image source: Martina Sprague.

As you continue your training, remember that, in a real self-defense situation, deep stabs to the midsection that houses the organs are generally more dangerous than stabs or slashes to the extremities. Slashes to primary targets, such as the throat or other areas that contain major blood vessels, can prove devastating. Surface slashes are less dangerous, but can produce a major psychological effect through heavy bleeding. It cannot be emphasized enough that knife attacks, when done with intent, come with a high degree of lethality also when undertaken by an untrained person.

Historical Gem: Knives are traditional combat weapons and have been carried by soldiers in armies the world over. The likelihood that the soldier on the battlefield will be forced to resort to the knife in combat has historically depended on the theater of operations and the culture of the belligerents. Agrarian societies, for example, have a greater history of edged weapon warfare than industrialized societies, particularly with respect to larger knives, such as machetes and bolos, which are frequently used as agricultural tools and therefore readily available to the local population, including rebel groups and guerrilla fighters. Large scale warfare, however, requires less stealth than skirmishes, particularly when the soldier can attack from a distance with a variety of missile weapons. Obviously, one cannot approach artillery with a knife, as proven in the devastation of World War I, when soldiers were sent forward with bayonets against firearms. Despite the uncertainty of encountering hand-to-hand combat, soldiers have relied on knife training in times of peace to enhance their skills in situations requiring immediate action on the field of battle. Knife training has traditionally emphasized attacking an unsuspecting enemy from the rear (as when stalking a sentry), or attacking and defending against an adversary in hand-to-hand combat at close range (as in trench warfare). Since the knife is a relatively simple weapon to master and requires skills mostly in the form of mental strength and aggression, the soldier's psychological training often proves more important than his physical training. Most untrained men can become lethal with almost any size and type of edged weapon, if they are willing and mentally ready to use it against their enemy. To reach proficiency with the knife, the recruit has historically received training not only in technicalities, such as holding the knife and cutting or stabbing from different angles, but, perhaps more importantly, in getting comfortable with the idea of using the knife with determination against an adversary. It is reasoned that sound training, coupled with the development of proper attitude, will make the soldier particularly formidable. The psychological effect that the feel of the knife has, and the weight of the steel in the hand, gives the soldier further confidence to carry out the attack. When faced with a determined knife-wielding soldier, an enemy combatant would likely choose flight if given the opportunity.

LESSON OBJECTIVES

Upon completion of this lesson, you should:

1. Have practiced your empty-hand martial arts stances, blocks, and strikes with and without a knife, and acquired insights into necessary adjustments to techniques and targets when wielding the knife

2. Have developed further understanding through technique practice of how the knife can be implemented into the grab and punch techniques and defenses taught in your empty-hand martial art

3. Have studied the targets normally attacked within your empty-hand martial art, and considered the extent to which they prove suitable for a knife attack

4. Have explored a multitude of defenses with the knife in forward and reverse grip against empty-handed attacks, and considered how a stab or slash to a primary target would end the fight

5. Have experimented with implementing the knife in the forms (kata) that are normally taught in your empty-hand martial art

A FEW POINTERS PRIOR TO TECHNIQUE PRACTICE

Common techniques learned in the stand-up martial arts include stances, strikes, kicks, blocks, and evasive movement. These techniques are then combined and further built upon during technique practice, forms practice, and sparring. When learning a new technique, it helps to break it down into its component parts and practice each segment separately. When wielding a knife, a good way to start is by blocking an empty-hand attack repeatedly by slashing your opponent's wrist, for example, before moving on to the full technique. Start stationary and have your partner attack with full forward momentum, to learn about timing and the importance of seizing the initiative through movement and action. While you might at first practice the technique stationary and in the air, to gain practical value, you must also train against a partner attacking at various speeds.

When you have learned a new technique, practice it on a regular basis. Granted, when you have learned a hundred techniques, it might not be possible to practice every one on a regular basis. But you can at least learn to recognize similarities between techniques. A *shuto* (knife hand strike, from hereon called a *shuto* to avoid confusing it with an edged weapon attack), for example, is used in many techniques. If you can do this strike empty-handed, can you also do it with a knife in your hand? To understand how different strikes tend to follow similar movement patterns, you might substitute one strike or target for another. For example, substitute a back fist to the temple with a finger whip to the eyes; or substitute a back fist to the temple with an outside forearm strike to the nose; or substitute a ridge hand to the groin with an open palm strike to the groin. The same principles apply when you pick up a knife and use essentially the same movement pattern as in your empty-hand technique. This is how previously learned muscle memory will aid your knife training.

If you can do a technique empty-handed . . .

. . . you can likely do it with a weapon in your hand, using the same hand motion or striking pattern. Image source: Martina Sprague.

Depending on the design, the knife can be used to stab, slash, trap or hook (with the spine), and strike (with the pommel). If the knife is of smaller design, it can easily be worked into your empty-hand techniques and striking patterns. Be aware that a knife is most dangerous when in motion. Keeping the knife in motion will therefore give you greater control of the situation by presenting a constant threat to your opponent and interfering with his attempts to disarm you. Only keep the knife stationary if the distance is such that your opponent can't reach you or your weapon. Be aware that knife disarming techniques typically taught in the training hall often assume that the attack will be clean, nearly stationary or in slow motion, and that the practitioner will be in possession of the fine motor skills required to disarm an adversary. When his life is threatened, however, this is unlikely the case. Thus, if you are the attacker and have access to a knife, keeping it in motion will interfere with your opponent's attempts to use the disarming skills he has learned in his empty-hand martial art.

Let's say that your opponent throws a straight strike to your head. An empty-hand defense might involve assuming a fighting stance and blocking the attack with a single or double forearm block to the inside of the opponent's arm. Although this move might prevent you from getting hit, we know by now that a simple defensive move is not enough to deter an opponent intent on doing damage. You can pretty much count on that he will throw a second strike. You must therefore seize the initiative and counterstrike before he does. Think of your block as a signal to launch your counterstrike. For instance, you might throw a back fist to your opponent's temple following your initial block. If you were holding a knife in your lead hand, you might slash his neck within the same movement pattern as the back fist following your initial block.

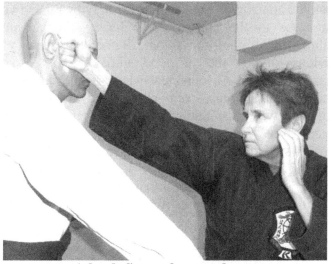

A back fist to the temple . . .

. . . follows essentially the same striking pattern as a knife slash to the neck. Image source: Martina Sprague.

Look for ways that seem natural for facilitating the speed of your counterstrike. For example, to increase the speed, block the attack with your forearm simply by raising your arm close to the side of your head, simultaneously slashing directly to the throat. Remember from your previous studies that a good initial target is your opponent's hand. An opponent who practices an empty-hand martial art must eventually extend a hand toward you, and will thus automatically present you with a target. Once you cut his hands, you will disable his "weapons." However, the hand is also a secondary target not designed to end the fight. If you can take a primary target instead, such as his throat, while protecting your own vital targets with your free hand or arm, it may lead you to victory quicker.

Your forearm can protect a large part of your body, and is therefore an efficient blocking weapon. By using your forearm to defend against an attack, you can block your opponent's strike and counterattack with the knife simultaneously. Image source: Martina Sprague.

Now, let's say that your opponent grabs your left wrist with his right hand, and your prescribed empty-hand defense calls for a right hammer fist strike to his wrist to release the grip, followed by a right back fist to the temple, a right front kick to the groin, and a right vertical punch to the nose. The same defense can be done with a knife against an opponent attacking empty-handed. Slight changes might be needed. For example, slash the throat instead of throwing a back fist to the temple.

Next, let's look at a grabbing rather than striking scenario. Let's say that you desire to place your opponent in a rear choke/sleeper hold. An effective escape from a sleeper hold is a forward throw over the shoulder. An attempted sleeper hold involving a knife (arm wrapped around opponent's neck and knife against his throat) can similarly be escaped though a forward throw with a simultaneous downward pull on the knife hand. Keeping your opponent's weight to the rear will complicate or totally negate his escape attempt. This can be accomplished, for example, by kicking the back of his knee as you wrap your arm around his neck. In fact, he may now be unable to move his upper body forward at all for fear of getting his throat cut.

The sleeper hold with the knife relies on the threat of cutting the throat, and not on choking as you would empty-handed. But the hold is essentially the same both empty-handed and with the knife, and many of the same principles, such as taking the opponent's balance, can be applied to prevent an escape. Image source: Martina Sprague.

Now, grip the knife and assume a neutral training stance, or alternatively a fighting stance that is typical of your martial art. Start with a single-edged knife and practice blocks and strikes, cutting edge facing your intended target. The forward grip is safer than the reverse grip in many ways, but primarily because it gives you reach without placing you within danger of your opponent's strikes. Be particularly observant when switching to reverse grip, ensuring that the dull edge is facing your forearm and the sharp edge the intended target. Which targets prove most suitable for a reverse grip knife attack? We often think of reverse grip as most suitable for slashing type attacks, but straight downward, upward, or sideways stabs also work well.

The reverse grip also allows you to use your hand for striking (the same hand in which you are holding the knife). Why would you want to strike with the hand that holds the knife, when in worst case scenario you might lose the weapon to your opponent? One reason is because it allows you to throw a few punches as a distraction from a longer distance prior to attacking with the knife (reverse grip requires a considerable distance closure). This may prevent your opponent from grabbing or otherwise tying up your knife hand.

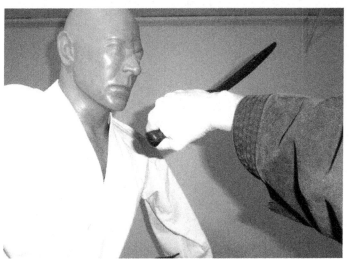

Jabbing your opponent may allow you to close the distance safely prior to cutting with the knife in reverse grip. Image source: Martina Sprague.

Now, from your training stance, hold the knife in reverse grip and practice passing the knife from your right to left hand and back again, until you can do so quickly and with ease. Make sure that the sharp edge is always aimed at your opponent. Repeat the exercise with the knife in forward grip. Although passing the knife from one hand to the other is not recommended for show, because it comes with the risk of losing the knife, the ability to pass the knife from one hand to the other might prevent your opponent from grabbing your knife hand and disarming you or otherwise restricting your mobility. In addition to giving you more versatility, the ability to pass the knife smoothly from one hand to the other can also make you more unpredictable. Skillfully passing the knife from one hand to the other may interfere with your opponent's ability to focus on the hand that holds the knife.

You can easily pass the knife from one hand the other by bringing your hands together at your centerline and ensuring that one hand always remains in contact with the knife. Image source: Martina Sprague.

Now that you have done some preparatory exercises with the knife, shadow boxing is a good warm-up exercise that helps you get in the right mind-set for the rest of the training session. Take a few minutes before the start of each workout and shadow box while wielding the knife. Work on correct execution of technique, using all strikes and grips you have learned in the previous books of the *Knife Training Methods and Techniques for Martial Artists* series. You might start doing each technique slow, with control and full extension. Be attentive to every movement of your body and any time your balance seems to suffer. Speed up and work on combining several stabs and slashes from forward and reverse grip. Involve your free hand in a blocking, parrying, grabbing, or striking fashion in conjunction with knife moves. Be constantly aware of the position of the knife and careful not to move your free hand into its path, risking inadvertent cuts to your own hand. Incorporate the kicks used in your empty-hand martial art. Remember that each combination must be logical. A quick slash with the knife in reverse grip, for instance, would prove illogical following a sidekick designed to set your opponent back. Why? Because the reverse grip slash is a short-range technique and cannot be executed properly following a sidekick, unless you first step forward to close the distance. Spinning back kicks or other spinning kicks are generally not practical when your intent is to cut with the knife, because these tend to take time to execute and require better balance and athletic ability than the basic front and roundhouse kicks. When engaged in a knife fight, the fastest and straightest way to reach your opponent is generally the best.

Now, then, that you have some idea of where we are headed, let's continue by exploring several empty-hand defenses commonly practiced in the stand-up martial arts and adapting these to the knife.

EMPTY-HAND AND KNIFE COMPARISONS IN STANCE PRACTICE

We often practice our basic strikes, kicks, and blocks from a horse stance (neutral stance) for warm-up and preparatory to other technique practice. Grab the knife in your dominant hand (right hand if you are right-handed) in the forward grip, and assume a horse stance the way you normally would in your empty-hand martial art. Run through all basic strikes, kicks, and blocks with the knife in your hand. When alternating sides; for instance, when doing an inward block with the right hand followed by an inward block with the left hand, the block with your right hand will be done with the knife, and the block with your left hand will be empty-handed. Previously learned muscle memory should make this exercise feel quite natural. Switch the knife to your weak hand (left hand if you are right-handed), and run through all the basic strikes, kicks, and blocks again. When adding kicks, and if your empty-hand martial art calls for high kicks and a pulling motion with the opposite hand, think about how you might implement the knife in this exercise. Could the pulling motion resemble a slashing block along your opponent's leg as he kicks, for instance? Now, switch the knife to reverse grip and run through all basic strikes, kicks, and blocks again. You might have to visualize different targets when working with the knife in reverse grip.

The basic blocks and strikes can be practiced through a pattern involving continuous motion, as demonstrated here: rising block, inward block, outward block, down and outward block, and straight thrust. Image source: Martina Sprague.

Now, with the knife in forward grip, do an inward block, imagining impacting your opponent's arm or hand with the lower third part of the blade for strength (near the handle). Consider whether you are holding a single- or double-edged knife. If single-edged, ensure that the sharp edge is turned toward your imaginary opponent's strike. How would you go from an inward block (toward your centerline) directly to an outward block (away from your centerline) with a single-edged knife? Turning the knife in your hand with the edge facing outward would probably be overly complicated. You might want to turn your whole hand instead (palm forward). When wielding a double-edged knife, by contrast, turning your hand palm forward, when transitioning from inward to outward block, is not absolutely necessary; although, it can be done. This exercise demonstrates the importance of cutting edge awareness when applying knife techniques to your empty-hand martial art.

When moving from inward to outward block with a single-edged knife, you must turn your hand palm forward to ensure that the cutting edge is facing your target (your opponent's arm). Image source: Martina Sprague.

When you have practiced from the horse stance, assume a right or left fighting stance (in some martial arts called a right or left bow stance). Start with the knife in your lead hand in forward grip. Some martial arts emphasize placing your stronger side forward, particularly if you rely on speed or touch sparring to score a point. The full contact arts tend to emphasize placing your stronger side to the rear, so that your rear hand has sufficient distance for building momentum for a powerful strike. Since the knife is a touch weapon, it is recommended that you fight with your knife hand forward primarily for speed and reach. This is not to say that placing your knife hand to the rear is wrong and, as you will discover, there are times when it will benefit you; for example, when concealing the knife or preventing an opponent from grabbing and controlling your weapon hand.

Run through all your basic strikes, kicks, and blocks from a fighting stance. This should give you a somewhat realistic view of how to implement the knife into your empty-hand martial arts techniques. Observe yourself in a mirror. Your strikes and blocks should preferably not extend outside of the boundaries of your body, because this would result in wasted motion. You also risk exposing targets to your opponent. If your martial art calls for keeping your nonworking hand by your hip, you might want to adjust it slightly by raising it high to the side of your neck, particularly if your imaginary opponent is also wielding a knife. Remember that the blood vessels in the neck are primary targets and a cut to these could end the fight instantly. Repeat the exercise with the knife in reverse grip. Then place the knife in your rear hand and repeat the exercise again from forward and reverse grip.

How you hold your hands when in your fighting stance may prove detrimental to your safety, particularly if your opponent is also armed with a knife. The neck is an important target to protect, because, as discussed in Book 4 of the *Knife Training Methods and Techniques for Martial Artists* series, the blood vessels in the neck are crucial for carrying blood to and from the brain, and are also near the surface of the skin, so even a nick to your neck with a sharp knife could end the fight. For this reason, you might want to adjust your hands to a high position near the sides of your neck, at least when within reach of your opponent, even if your martial art calls for a different hand position. Also think about how to move the knife from one side of your body to the other to protect against a strike or kick combination, without jeopardizing the integrity of your stance.

Now, observe yourself in the mirror. Your fighting stance should demonstrate combat presence; you should look as though you are ready to engage your opponent. When armed with a knife, however, it is not obvious that you want to brandish it from the start. You might choose to conceal it in reverse grip behind your forearm, which would require a non-threatening stance. But, whichever stance you choose, your mind should be combat ready; you should be prepared to brandish the knife and use it in defense against your opponent's attack. It has been said that the best defense is offense, despite the fact that the martial arts are popularly promoted as self-*defense*. As emphasized repeatedly throughout the *Knife Training Methods and Techniques for Martial Arts* series, to prove effective you must practice both offense and defense. The way you carry yourself when faced with a threat may determine whether you will be a winner or a victim.

Some people equate proper attitude with confidence. You can also think of it as combat presence.

Fighting stance showing combat readiness, and fighting stance with knife concealed behind forearm. Image source: Martina Sprague.

Next, assume a fighting stance with your knife hand to the front. In your empty-hand martial art, you are probably using both hands together in different blocking, parrying, and striking patterns. For instance, you might do an inward block or parry with your lead hand, followed by a straight strike with your rear hand. If the knife is in your lead hand, you will now block with the knife to your opponent's arm and follow with a rear hand strike. Since the arm is a secondary target not likely to end the fight, to make better use of the knife you might also block and immediately extend your arm, slashing your opponent's neck, allowing your knife hand to lead the attack as you follow with a rear hand strike to reinforce the knife attack and end the fight.

Knife Training Methods and Techniques for Martial Artists

A block to a secondary target such as the arm . . .

. . . can be followed by an immediate slash to a primary target such as the neck.

Upon retrieval of the knife, throw a rear hand punch to the jaw to down your opponent and end the fight. Image source: Martina Sprague.

A stable stance that facilitates ease of movement is important in empty-hand martial arts, and equally important the moment you pick up a knife or other weapon. If you are off balance or unable to move with ease, you cannot utilize a weapon to its fullest potential, and might also place yourself in jeopardy of your opponent's strikes or grab attempts. In empty-hand martial arts, you deprive your strikes of power the moment your stance is even a little unstable, or the moment your body lacks coordination. Because of the sharpness of the blade and the minimal amount of force it takes to inflict damage with a knife, body rotation for power is not as crucial when wielding the knife. But a bit of body rotation certainly doesn't harm, and will also help you stay true to the principles of your martial art.

Examine how your stance affects your ability to step forward, back, and to the side with speed and efficiency. You must seize the initiative; in other words, be first, particularly if your opponent is also wielding a weapon. Experiment with the best width of your stance. Many martial arts employ a medium wide/medium high stance; that is, with your feet approximately shoulder-width and a half apart. This may or may not prove comfortable when wielding the knife, and a small adjustment may prove necessary. If your martial art employs very low or wide stances, it might hinder mobility when you begin working with the knife in specific techniques or free sparring. If your stance hinders speed and movement, what necessary adjustments can you make that are still true to your martial art? If you normally employ very low stances, perhaps you can compromise and straighten your legs a bit?

Thus, although a low stance gives you stability, it could also inhibit movement. There may be times when a very low and wide stance benefits you, however. The so-called low crouch can be used successfully in knife fighting in preparation for cutting an adversary's legs. Furthermore, when blocking with the knife, use all blocks as if they were strikes in order to inflict as much damage as possible. For example:

1. When the threat is imminent but before it is immediate, hide the knife at your side.

2. As your opponent approaches, and it is clear that you will have to fight, assume a low crouch stance with the knife in reverse grip and the blade facing your opponent.

3. Your free hand should be close to your neck for protection.

4. From the low crouch, you can now drop straight down with the blade of the knife against your opponent's shin to block a sidekick or front kick aimed at your legs.

The low crouch stance can prove useful in preparation for an attack to the opponent's legs. Image source: Martina Sprague.

A good way to increase reach and power from a right or left fighting stance in empty-hand martial arts is by pivoting your feet, hips, and body in the direction of the strike (in some martial arts this is called a forward or reverse bow stance). You can also lunge, taking a step forward with your lead foot only, elongating your body for greater reach. But, as already discussed in relation to the fencer's thrust, you must not lunge too deeply, or you may not be able to retrieve the knife to the point of origin in time to defend against a counterattack. Unlike a sport fencer who is concerned only with scoring a point, a knife-wielding martial artist might have to use more than one strike to end the fight. A very deep lunge might deprive you of mobility and jeopardize your ability to execute several strikes in succession at a time when it is particularly crucial to retain speed and flexibility in your foundation.

Experiment with your stance to find a lunge that is optimum for mobility and reach. Image source: Martina Sprague.

Try also a series of shuffle steps until nearly within reach of your adversary before extending your knife arm. Aim at a specific target, such as the throat, chest, or midsection (view yourself in the mirror when working without a practice partner).

When holding the knife in reverse grip, you can still rotate your feet, hips, and body in the direction of the strike, but the move will no longer resemble the fencer about to score a touch. Imagine throwing a punch straight toward the target (your opponent's chin, for example). Now, with the knife in reverse grip, by aiming the punch slightly to the side of the chin, you will slash your opponent's throat. Nothing but the target has changed.

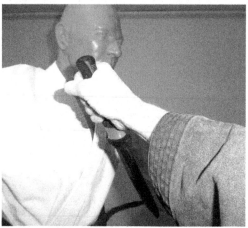

When slashing the throat with the knife in reverse grip, think about the motion of throwing a punch with full body rotation, but aim slightly to the side of the chin. The sharp edge of the knife will now impact the throat. Image source: Martina Sprague.

If holding the knife in your rear hand instead, you must be significantly closer to your opponent in order to reach him, but the rear hand grip also comes with certain benefits. For example, you can parry an attack with your empty lead hand while preventing an adversary from grabbing or controlling your knife hand. You can also conceal the knife easier in your rear hand while keeping your opponent occupied with your lead hand, interfering with his movement. As soon as you have blocked or parried with your lead hand, extend your rear hand and stab or slash to a vital target.

Now that you have some idea how to use the knife from lead and rear hand as you advance on your adversary, use these concepts when practicing your martial art stances. For instance you might go from a neutral fighting stance to a forward or reverse bow stance. The forward bow stance resembles the lunge, although not as deep, and gives you reach with the knife in forward grip. The reverse bow stance lends itself to an upward stab with the knife in reverse grip to your opponent's groin or abdomen.

The forward bow stance is done with the knife in your rear hand and resembles the lunge, but is not as deep. If this stance were done empty-handed, it would lend itself to a reverse strike. Image source: Martina Sprague.

The reverse bow stance lends itself to an upward stab to the abdomen or groin. If this stance were done empty-handed, it would lend itself to an upward hammer fist strike to the groin. Image source: Martina Sprague.

The reverse bow stance involves a pivot in your foot, hip, and body away from your opponent to increase the power in the upward strike, or to position your upper body out of reach of a counterstrike. Again, practice with the knife in your lead and rear hand, in forward and reverse grip. For example, with the knife in your lead hand forward grip, slash upward from a reverse bow stance. With the knife in your rear hand forward grip, use the knife as a shield or check against an oncoming attack from a reverse bow stance. With the knife in your lead hand reverse grip, enact a deep stab to your opponent's gut or groin area. With the knife in your rear hand reverse grip, use it as a shield or check or, if very close, slash your opponent's wrist when he extends his arm toward you.

Next, work on combining basic strikes, kicks, and blocks while moving from neutral to forward and reverse bow stances. Remember to use your free hand as a check or strike to reinforce your knife technique or deter your opponent's focus away from the knife. Try an upward block with the knife in reverse grip as defense against an overhead attack, followed by a reverse bow stance and an upward stab to opponent's abdomen. Or, try a downward block to opponent's strike or kick with the knife in forward grip, followed by a slash to his throat in the motion of an upward block. This is how you begin to incorporate your knife techniques into your empty-hand martial art without altering the basic characteristics of the art, while building on already acquired muscle memory.

Place a knife in reverse grip in each hand and experiment with different stabs, slashes, and movement patterns. Image source: Martina Sprague.

When you have practiced the forward and reverse bow stance in conjunction with knife strikes, it is time to explore how to advance (take ground, or press the attack) preparatory to landing a strike, and after landing a strike in preparation for a new attack. To retain balance, you will normally step with the foot closest to the direction of travel first, and readjust the width of your stance with your rear foot. When stepping forward, step with your lead foot first; when stepping back, step with your rear foot first. When stepping left, step with your left foot first; when stepping right, step with your right foot first. This ensures that you will never end up in a crossed stance that might jeopardize your balance. That is not to say that a crossed stance is necessarily wrong, but it should be used with reservation and viewed as a transitory stance. You may also use the crossed stance in preparation for throwing a kick, such as a crossover sidekick. If deciding to use a crossover or twist stance when advancing on your opponent, consider how it might be used as an aid for short-range fighting. Can you use your knees as checks against your opponent's foundation to control his movement and balance, for example? Also try slashing with the knife simultaneously to moving through the crossed stance.

What other stances does your empty-hand martial art teach that you can use effectively when armed with a knife? There are so-called "in-between" stances, required for repositioning yourself in preparation for a strike or kick. Switching stance in the middle of an engagement can prove productive and comes with several benefits. Offensively, it makes it more difficult for an adversary to anticipate your techniques. Defensively, it allows you to protect a part of your body that has been injured. When switching stance, be very careful not to expose targets on your centerline. You can switch stance while moving forward or back; however, moving forward, or taking ground, generally gives you the initiative and forces your opponent to backpedal, but this may or may not be true when wielding a knife.

If your opponent is also armed and you must avoid his strike, moving back might prove the better alternative. But remember that it may also place you out of range for counterstriking, and may thus make you lose valuable time. It is also possible to avoid an attack by stepping forward and jamming your opponent's arm, preventing him from using it or any handheld weapon against you. When switching stance, practice blocking an attack with the blade of the knife simultaneously, or, if within reach, stabbing or slashing a primary target intended to end the fight.

Deception is also an aspect of the martial arts, so it will benefit you to learn how to switch stance or switch the knife from one hand to the other smoothly and within other movement to conceal your intentions. However, wielding the knife with your lead hand is a good way to start, because of the many benefits it gives you in reaching and attacking an adversary before he has the opportunity to close distance. The unpredictability of a street encounter should prompt you to develop both sides of your body. Ultimately, the purpose of stance is to give you stability, power, and ease of movement.

Historical Gem: Seventeenth century Japanese swordsman Miyamoto Musashi, who was often involved in sword fights to the death, emphasized stance and movement practice, until it became as natural as walking. The skilled martial artist thus develops knowledge of himself until he sees things clearly and avoids getting caught up in emotions. Anger clouds the mind and should not rule your actions, nor should other biases. When the practice of martial arts remains a normal undertaking, you can act as you would on any normal day. This is how you achieve unity of body and mind. By showing neither overconfidence nor fear, you avoid exposing your intentions to the opponent. This is also how you avoid being deceived by the opponent's appearance. A big opponent is not necessarily strong, nor is a small opponent necessarily weak. You will thus be prepared to meet any challenge. Your martial arts stance should reflect this inwardly calm; it should neither be threatening nor timid, yet ready to meet any danger. When your combat stance is as natural as possible, you can live each day normally as if there were no dangers, yet always be ready for battle. Assuming a stance with your guard high when someone offends you may not only escalate an encounter, but give your opponent plenty of warning to ready his forces. Assuming a normal stance, by contrast, brings uncertainty to the mind of the opponent. He will not know when or how you will attack.

As you can see, there are many uses of the knife from the basic martial arts stances, and you are encouraged to experiment within the framework of your particular martial art. The idea is to use the knife as an empty-hand enhancement tool. Previously learned techniques and previously developed muscle memory should aid you in gaining proficiency quickly.

EMPTY-HAND AND KNIFE COMPARISONS IN BLOCKING PRACTICE

When blocking in your empty-hand martial art, all blocks should be thought of as strikes. The role of defense is two-fold: to protect you from harm, and to harm your opponent and set up counterstrikes. Likewise, when blocking with the knife, all blocks should be thought of as strikes. Your objective is to end the fight in the fewest number of moves possible. For example:

1. When the threat is imminent but not yet immediate, hide the knife by your side.

2. When it is clear that you can no longer avoid the fight, deploy the knife and assume a stance that feels comfortable to you with the knife in forward or reverse grip, based on the martial art you have practiced. Forward grip gives you greater reach and may also present a greater threat to your opponent. Reverse grip allows you to hide the knife behind your forearm until you are at close range and ready to use it.

3. Hold the knife in your lead hand, preferably, but this is not a hard and fast rule. Although lead hand deployment gives you greater reach and potentially greater protection, there are advantages to holding the knife in your rear hand; for example, easier concealment and less risk of getting disarmed.

4. Keep your free hand close to your body for protection, preferably by your neck, particularly if your opponent is also wielding a knife.

Now, then, that you are ready to receive your opponent's attack, use the part of the blade closest to the handle for a strong and solid block. Using the part closest to the tip will cut and do damage, but it is also the weaker part of the blade and may not be sturdy enough to block a full force attack from a forward grip position. If wielding a long blade, you will also have a long lever arm, and using the part closest to the tip may cause the knife to get twisted from your hand on impact with the target. If your intent is to slash your opponent's wrist rather than block, a nick with the tip of the blade may have shock value and could also afford you significant reach. But a deeper slash, starting from the thicker and sturdier part of the blade, will do more damage.

Second, be aware of the strengths and weaknesses inherent to the type of blade you are using. You can find more information about different blade designs in Book 1, *Knife Anatomy*, of the *Knife Training Methods and Techniques for Martial Artists* series. A single-edged knife held in the forward grip should be held with the cutting edge down. If you're not well practiced in deploying this type of knife, you risk deploying it with the cutting edge up. Blocking an attack with the normal inward block would then cause the dull edge of the knife (or the spine) to impact the target. Although this may stop the attack, it will violate the second principle of good defense: to harm your opponent simultaneous to blocking.

When blocking with a single-edged knife from forward grip with the cutting edge up, the spine will impact the target. Although this may halt the initial attack, it fails the second principle of good defense: to harm your opponent. Image source: Martina Sprague.

Third, the smaller the knife is, the less effective it is for blocking a full force attack. However, the smaller the knife is, the easier it is to conceal, so there is a tradeoff. A block with a big blade, by contrast, can prove quite crude; although, a big knife is also capable of producing a more devastating cut.

There are thus several strengths and weaknesses inherent

to blocking an attack with the blade of the knife. But what about blocking with the pommel, using a hammer fist motion with the knife held in forward grip?

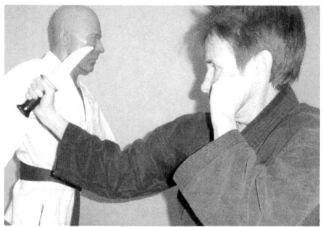

A benefit of blocking a strike with the pommel is that a lot of force can be concentrated into this relatively small surface area. Another benefit is that you can rely on the natural motion of the hammer fist strike. A drawback is that it requires considerably more precision than blocking with the blade, and that it will not do as much damage as slashing the target. Image source: Martina Sprague.

No defensive move should be considered in isolation. Each defensive move is a tactic designed to take you closer to victory. Defense must therefore be followed by offense. For instance, block the strike with the sharp edge of the blade and, immediately as the block has served its purpose (to protect you from harm and inflict damage on your opponent's striking weapon), follow with a strike to a vital target, such as a slash to his throat or side of neck. If the adversary strikes downward with a stick or knife, the same principle applies. You might use an upward block, impacting his wrist or arm with the sharp edge of the blade. Follow with a slash to his throat or side of neck, or drop to one knee after blocking the attack and slash the large blood vessels on his inside thigh area. A stab to a vital target can also be used as a finishing technique.

Try this for a simple block and counter against a strike, empty-handed first and then with the knife: Inward block or hammer fist strike to opponent's forearm followed by a back fist to the temple. Now with the knife in either forward or reverse grip, block or slash opponent's forearm or wrist, followed by a stab to his throat or neck. The motion of the knife is nearly identical to the motion of your fist in the empty-handed defense. When you have practiced a number of common blocks and counterstrikes with a knife, go back to doing them empty-handed. But think about them as if you were still holding the knife. This exercise builds confidence and precision.

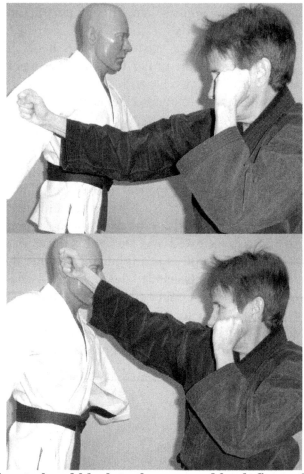

Empty-hand block to the arm and back fist to the temple. Image source Martina Sprague.

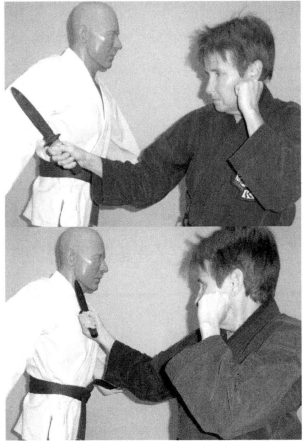

**Block with knife in forward grip and stab to the neck.
Image source: Martina Sprague.**

**Block with knife in reverse grip and stab to the neck.
Image source: Martina Sprague.**

It seems natural to block as an initial counter to an attack and follow with a slash or stab, as explored repeatedly in the *Knife Training Methods and Techniques for Martial Artists* series. But since we will use the knife as a martial art enhancement tool; in other words, we will incorporate it into regular empty-handed martial arts techniques, you might also want to consider using a kick as an initial counter to an attack. Start in front of the heavy bag and visualize your opponent throwing a strike. Use open handed parries or slaps to defend against the initial swing and set up offense. Consider how you might design a technique that flows smoothly from a defensive parry to an offensive kick. If you have practiced your kicks in sparring, you will know that only certain kicks can be thrown effectively following a defensive hand technique. Distance is an important consideration. For instance, if you parry a punch and step forward and slightly to the side of your opponent, you may be too close for throwing a front kick, sidekick, or spinning back kick effectively, while a roundhouse kick may work just fine. The same applies if you are armed with a knife. If you block your opponent's strike with the sharp edge of the blade and step forward and slightly to the side, you will likely find that a front kick, sidekick, or spinning back kick will not work as well, distance-wise, as a roundhouse kick. You must also keep your objective in mind: how to finish the fight. While a sidekick can prove superbly powerful and break a rib or knock your opponent off balance, additional distance closure after the kick lands may be required if you wish to finish the fight with the knife.

Now, then, practice with a partner in light contact free sparring, blocking his strikes with the sharp edge of the knife and countering with a kick (using a martial arts practice knife, of course). Make sure the kick is suitable for the distance. Kick to targets where you are likely to inflict significant damage (use no or very light contact with your training partner). Throwing low kicks to the legs or groin allows you to maintain your foundation and avoid telegraphing the kicks. It also prevents your opponent from grabbing your kicking leg. Any kick that turns your body to an awkward position may not be the best kick for knife fighting. For instance, rather than throwing the sidekick, throw the stop kick (with your body facing forward and your foot turned to the outside). Not only can the stop kick be thrown with greater ease and accuracy, it is powerful and allows you to maintain your forward momentum.

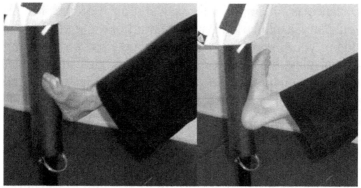

Sidekick with foot turned to the inside (toward your centerline) vs. stop kick with foot turned to the outside (away from your centerline). The stop kick can be thrown effectively to the knees to stop an opponent's advance. Since the motion of your upper body is identical to the motion involved when throwing a front kick, the stop kick can be thrown with forward momentum behind it and without telegraphing it to your opponent. Image source: Martina Sprague.

EMPTY-HAND AND KNIFE COMPARISONS IN TARGET PRACTICE

As emphasized repeatedly in the *Knife Training Methods and Techniques for Martial Artists* series, the use of a knife in a confrontation can have devastating results. Stabbing or slashing to specific targets can quickly prove lethal. A philosophical aim of some martial arts is to use the art only in defense and do no more damage than is necessary. However, defending yourself with a knife without severely injuring or killing your opponent may not prove possible when attacking primary targets, such as the eyes, neck, heart, organs contained in the midsection (liver, kidney, spleen, stomach, intestines), or major blood vessels. Even a cut to the Achilles tendon, although probably not lethal, can have a devastating effect. If your opponent is wearing thick clothing, some of these targets may prove difficult to reach.

Target accuracy with the knife can at first be practiced on a focus mitt. You will most likely find that stabbing is more difficult than slashing with accuracy, because slashing automatically takes a bigger target. After training on a focus mitt, practice on a cardboard box marked with specific targets. For more lifelike practice, you might want to get a Styrofoam head. Styrofoam mannequin heads designed to hold wigs can be purchased inexpensively online. A martial arts dummy bag will also work. In addition to targets for stabs (eyes, heart, midsection, etc.), remember that there are four major targets for slashes, with several subtle variations. These major targets are:

1. The back of the hands

2. The wrists

3. The blood vessels on both sides of the neck

4. The large blood vessels on the inner thighs

When practicing with a training knife in the air, on a dummy, or on a partner, avoid flailing the knife. Each cut should be aimed at a precise target. Although you can probably inflict damage also if you are flailing the knife or striking targets randomly, as with all martial arts techniques, precision results in safety, speed, and endurance, because it eliminates unnecessary or large moves that extend outside the boundaries of your body and that expose vital targets to your opponent. The skilled martial artist uses a calculated calmness; flailing is a sign of fear and inexperience.

That said, when first learning the moves of a specific technique, whether empty-handed or with a knife, you might use slightly exaggerated moves until your body adjusts to the new demands placed on it. But your goal should be to tighten the moves and strike with precision, until all unnecessary motion is eliminated. A stab should be aimed at a precise target and be straight and deep, after which the knife should be withdrawn quickly. Think point of origin. When throwing a strike in your empty-hand martial art, your hand is not left on target or lazily dropped to your side, but is returned to point of origin. Why? So that you can defend your openings and throw another strike, if need be.

You have probably identified several strikes and targets that prove effective for ending a fight in your empty-hand martial art. Now, do the same with your knife techniques. Generally, any area where skin is exposed can be targeted. Slashing the hand that is striking or grabbing you can prove useful for seizing the initiative and turning the odds in your favor, particularly if your opponent is unknowing of the fact that you have a knife. You can still launch additional attacks to primary targets, but you may not need to if release and escape are your objectives. Your empty-hand martial art might also have taught you how to grab your opponent's clothing, hair, arm, or other body part, and manipulate him into position to expose critical targets. Experiment with these same moves for your knife techniques. For example, can you expose a target on his neck by grabbing his hair and tilting his head?

You have probably also used *shutos* in your empty-hand martial art (also called knife hand strikes) to reach targets that are otherwise difficult to reach, such as the throat or back of neck. Or, you might have used *shutos* for focus of power, because of the ease with which they conform to the shape of certain targets, such as the floating ribs. Identify narrow targets on your opponent's body; for instance, the space between the ribs, and explore how you might manipulate the knife to conform to these targets, to avoid having to cut through bone. Which is easiest: turning your hand palm up or palm down when armed with a knife and stabbing between the ribs?

Palm up or palm down? Experiment with the best way to stab with precision between the ribs. Image source: Martina Sprague.

When exploring target precision with the knife, you might also start by identifying the types of strikes (closed and open fist) and targets you normally use in your empty-hand martial art. Grab the knife in forward grip and explore how to reach these same targets with the knife. What is the best way to reach the neck? Should you use an inward or outward slash, or an inward or outward stab? Why? Identify targets on your opponent's arms, such as his armpit, biceps, crook of the elbow, and wrist, and think about situations when you might attack these with the knife. Choose a technique from your empty-hand martial art: a wrist or shoulder grab, for instance. When your opponent grabs your wrist, can you cut his hand or wrist without risking a cut to your own hand? How about a stab to his armpit as defense against a wrist or lapel grab? What type of defense do you normally use empty-handed to release the grip? How would you use the knife while still staying within the basic pattern of your empty-hand technique?

A stab to the armpit can prove devastating to an opponent who reaches out to grab you. Image source: Martina Sprague.

Continue identifying targets on the torso that you would normally strike empty-handed, such as the sternum, solar plexus, liver, or kidneys. Do the same with the legs. If you normally don't strike to the legs, perhaps there is a technique that calls for a kick to the legs; either inside or outside thigh area or knee, and the groin for sure. When you have explored how to implement the use of the knife in forward grip within the confines of your empty-hand technique, switch to reverse grip and start again, exploring techniques and targets on the head, torso, arms, and legs. Can you reach these targets also if you are not standing directly in front of your adversary? When you have finished a technique, does your martial art call for a specific way in which to distance yourself from your opponent? When distancing yourself in your empty-hand martial art, it is a good idea to take something with you; for example, a handful of hair or skin. How can you take something with you within the movement of distancing yourself from your adversary when wielding a knife? We talked a bit about angling out in Book 8 of the *Knife Training Methods and Techniques for Martial Artists* series. Angling out allows you to attain a superior position away from your opponent's attack line. It also allows you to slash a target that may drop him to the ground, such as the tendons at the back of the knee.

Giving your opponent multiple points of pain inhibits his ability to respond and counterstrike. One strike to one target (one point of pain) is easier to defend against than multiple strikes to diverse targets. For instance, after defending against the initial attack in empty-hand martial arts, strike with a back fist to the temple and then with a front kick to the groin. You have a greater chance landing the front kick if you strike with the back fist first, because your opponent is still absorbed in the pain from the back fist by the time the front kick lands, and he will not know which target to defend next. When wielding a knife, you can likewise think of primary and secondary targets. First, strike a secondary target intended to stop your opponent's strike (his wrist, for instance). Then, strike a primary target intended to end the fight (his throat, for instance). By the time the knife strikes his throat, he is still thinking about the slash to his wrist, and perhaps the fact that you have disarmed him. The initiative is now yours.

EMPTY-HAND AND KNIFE COMPARISONS IN STRIKING AND KICKING PRACTICE

Although body rotation for power is not as crucial when wielding a knife as it is in empty-hand martial arts, some pivot might still give you increased reach. A proper pivot can also help you strike straight. A drawback is that it could potentially increase the time it takes to strike, because of the energy and time required to move your body instead of just your arm. Although you should generally pivot your body for power and reach when throwing an empty-hand strike, whether lead or rear hand, you can do a quick stab successfully with the knife in your lead hand without pivoting.

It is still a good idea to explore pivots when using the knife in conjunction with empty-hand techniques. A pivot could potentially give you more space to execute a technique. For example, an upward stab to your opponent's groin or gut, when done in conjunction with a reverse bow pivot, places your upper body at a safer distance from your adversary and turns it in a direction that facilitates escape.

Reverse bow pivot with a stab to the groin or gut gives you distance and facilitates escape. Image source: Martina Sprague.

Bringing your hand back to point of origin after throwing a strike is yet an important concept in empty-hand martial arts, because it protects the openings you have left on your body as a result of extending your arm, and prepares you for throwing a follow-up strike with the same hand, or with the other hand without experiencing a contradiction in body mechanics. When wielding the knife, you may or may not bring your hand back to point of origin, depending on whether you intend to take the same target several times or different targets in rapid succession (such as a slash to your opponent's throat followed by a stab to his abdomen). If using your free hand as part of the technique, your knife hand must work in coordination with your free hand. More often than not, extending both of your arms together does not prove beneficial to movement, balance, and power. Getting your knife hand grabbed and disarmed would also prove disastrous.

The question is how to use your free hand while working with the knife. We already know that it is important to protect your neck against a potential knife attack, but many martial arts call for carrying one hand high and one low in order to defend against a high or low strike or kick, while protecting as many openings as possible. When deciding how to carry your free hand, start by staying within the established patterns of your martial art. After some practice and analysis, you can make the changes that seem the most beneficial.

With the previous in mind, note how many of your empty-hand strikes resemble knife strikes in the movement patterns of your body and limbs. For instance, take the different types of elbow strikes. Start with the horizontal elbow. With the knife in reverse grip, note how the exact movement you used in the elbow strike allows you to slash with the knife in an inward fashion (toward your centerline). What about the upward elbow strike? Again, you can utilize the exact same movement pattern with a knife in reverse grip. Even the distance is nearly identical. The downward elbow strike, when wielding a knife in reverse grip, requires some extension of your arm, but otherwise the movement is essentially the same.

The horizontal elbow and inward slash with the knife in reverse grip follow essentially the same movement pattern. Image source: Martina Sprague.

The upward elbow and upward slash with the knife in reverse grip follow essentially the same movement pattern. Image source: Martina Sprague.

The downward elbow and downward stab with the knife in reverse grip follow essentially the same movement pattern. Image source: Martina Sprague.

Look at similar movement patterns between empty-hand and knife in other strikes and blocks that are part of your empty-hand martial art; for instance, the empty-hand inward block or hammer fist strike. Note how the move compares to a slashing attack when armed with a knife in forward grip, and a stabbing attack when armed with the knife in reverse grip.

The empty-hand inward block or hammer fist strike

utilizes essentially the same body mechanics as a downward slash with the knife in forward grip . . .

. . . or a downward stab with the knife in reverse grip. Image source: Martina Sprague.

From a neutral stance (horse stance), practice the strike variations typically found in your martial art. You have probably learned a number of straight strikes, such as lock punch and snap punch. You have probably also learned several other variations, such as back fist, hammer fist, and *shuto* (knife hand strike), in addition to a variety of elbow strikes. Train with the knife in forward and reverse grip and observe how the angle to the target, or the target itself, might change slightly depending on which type of grip you use. This is an excellent opportunity for using a martial arts training dummy resembling a real person. For instance, a back fist type strike with the knife in forward grip could give you an outward slashing type movement (it could also give you a stabbing movement if you turn your hand palm up). Several targets lend themselves to this type of attack; for example, side of neck, biceps, or wrist. A back fist type strike with the knife in reverse grip could also resemble a slashing attack, if you turn your hand palm up. You can also stab within the back fist movement by turning your hand palm down.

The hammer fist strike proves particularly practical through its resemblance to a downward or diagonal stab with the knife in reverse grip, or a slash with the knife in the forward grip. The hammer fist movement might be the most natural to perform also for an untrained person. Even a toddler with no martial arts training whatsoever can normally throw strikes resembling the hammer fist.

The uppercut can likewise be thrown with a knife in your hand; for example, by slashing tightly upward and slightly diagonally to your opponent's throat. Try it from forward and reverse grip.

The uppercut and upward and outward slash with the knife in reverse grip resemble each other in motion. Image source: Martina Sprague.

So, how would you use the knife in conjunction with basic kicks? As already discussed briefly, remember that kicks in combinations must be logical to be of value. In other words, if you use a kick intended to set your opponent back, such as a sidekick or spinning back kick, it would prove illogical to follow it with a short-range technique, such as a knee strike or a hand technique, unless you are well prepared to close the distance first. Since the knife is held in your hand, you can think of it as a hand technique, even though it gives you marginally longer reach than an empty hand. The same principle therefore applies; in other words, it would prove illogical to throw a kick intended to set your opponent back, and follow it with a knife attack. It would be better to throw a kick that keeps your opponent in place, such as a roundhouse kick to his legs, prior to the knife attack. Kicks designed to set your opponent back can be used as finishing techniques both when empty-handed and when deploying a knife. Now, throw kicks in combinations as you advance across the floor. When you think you have achieved a logical combination, try it on a cooperative partner.

Kicks can also come in handy when switching stance. A front kick with you rear leg, for instance, planting that leg forward, allows you to switch stance while simultaneously engaging in offense. If the knife is in your rear hand, a kick with your rear leg, whether intended for damage or as a fake, can help you place your rear side forward and make your opponent focus on the kick instead of the knife. Your rear hand has now become your lead hand; in other words, the knife is now in your lead hand, even though there was no hand change involved. Low kicks to the legs can also prove valuable distractions for switching stance or attaining a position more suitable for a knife attack. It is thus advisable to throw a strike or kick (or to cut or block with the knife) simultaneous to switching stance to distract your opponent and hinder him from blocking or grabbing your knife arm.

After identifying kicks that prove suitable for use in conjunction with knife techniques, explore how to use a knife attack in combination with these kicks, whether prior to throwing the kick or after the kick has landed. You might also use the knife as part of a longer combination involving both strikes and kicks. For example, if your adversary grabs your wrist, and you normally respond with a hammer fist strike to his wrist to break the grip, followed by a back fist to the temple, a front kick to the groin, and a vertical strike to the nose; with the knife in forward grip, you might now substitute the hammer fist for a slash to his wrist, the back fist for a slash across the throat (or a stab to the throat if you turn your hand palm up, or a strike to the temple with the pommel). Keep the front kick to the groin as prescribed, and then stab to the midsection.

Many martial arts schools also teach "one-step" sparring, where one student is the aggressor and the other the defender. Your sparring partner might do a predetermined technique (a front kick, for example), which you must defend against with a predetermined defense (a downward block). When you gain some experience, you can speed up your predetermined blocks and counters until they become free flowing and natural. Or, you might practice one-step sparring using random techniques. Try the following with a knife in your dominant hand:

1. Student A does any technique, and student B uses any type of defense.

2. After student B has blocked the attack, he or she throws a counterattack.

3. Student A now blocks and counters. The exercise starts again.

EMPTY-HAND AND KNIFE COMPARISONS IN GRAB TECHNIQUE DEFENSES

In all of the following techniques, it is assumed that you are right-handed and hold the knife in your right hand. The opponent is empty-handed. If you are left-handed, hold the knife in your left hand and perform the mirror image of the techniques as described. The purpose is to explore how you can use the empty-hand defenses you have learned also when wielding a knife. This allows you to build on already established muscle memory which, in turn, allows you to enhance the techniques you already know by adding speed and the devastation inherent to wielding an edged weapon. Although the knife is dangerous also when wielded by an untrained person, and any crudely executed stab or slash can end a fight, after years of practicing your martial art, you may want to add some finesse in accord with the principles of fighting you have already learned.

Single Wrist Grab

Empty-Hand: Opponent grabs your left wrist with his right hand in an attempt to control you, pull you along, or hold you steady and in range for a strike with his other hand. As with any defense, your chances of success increase if you react before he achieves a firm grip, and otherwise as soon as possible after he grabs you. The best time to act is while his focus is on grabbing you, but before he thinks of his follow-up move. A possible empty-handed defense against the wrist grab involves turning your hand palm up to expose the weaknesses in your opponent's fingers, simultaneously stepping forward with your right foot and dropping your weight in conjunction with a right hammer fist strike to his wrist. This is designed to release the grip. But releasing the grip is not enough. You must also counter to ensure that he will not attempt to grab you anew. A possible counterstrike is a right back fist to the temple. If you can split your opponent's focus so that he must defend several targets at the same time, your chances of reaching safety will increase. You might therefore throw a front kick to the groin after landing the back fist to the temple. His natural reaction is to bend his upper body forward or drop at the knees. This is a good time to throw a straight right punch to the nose, while the forward motion of his upper body meets the momentum of your strike. As you can see, all strikes in this suggested defense against the wrist grab are done with your right side; in this case, lead hand or foot for speed. Now, grab the knife in forward grip with your right hand (mirror the technique if you are left-handed).

Knife Forward Grip: You can still turn your hand palm up to expose your opponent's fingers when he grabs your wrist. But instead of throwing a hammer fist strike, slash across his wrist or forearm. Then strike with the pommel to the temple, or alternatively, slash across the throat. Follow with a front kick to the groin (same as in your empty-hand defense). As his upper body comes forward, stab straight to the abdomen. As you can see, you have stayed almost precisely within the pattern of your empty-hand defense. Only the targets have changed slightly. Now, switch the knife to reverse grip and repeat.

Knife Reverse Grip: Although you could stab to your

adversary's wrist, a stab may prove difficult since you're under a lot of stress, and precision is key. Try instead a slight upward slash to the wrist. Follow with a stab to the right side of the neck, and then a front kick to the groin. As his upper body comes forward, slash upward (as if you're throwing an upward elbow strike) and slightly diagonally outward to the throat. Again, the targets have changed slightly, but you still remain largely within the pattern of the original technique, which means that you can rely on previously learned muscle memory. Note that this is just a suggested defense against the wrist grab. Work on it if you like it; otherwise use one that is particular to your martial art while staying within the basic pattern of the original technique.

Cross Wrist Grab

Empty-Hand: Opponent grabs your right wrist with his right hand in a cross wrist grab. Your empty-hand defense calls for twisting your hand under and to the outside of your opponent's hand, grabbing his wrist. Simultaneously, step forward to a left fighting stance and strike with a left inward block to the back of his elbow to hyperextend his arm, pulling your right hand toward you and pushing with your left forearm against the back of his elbow to bend his upper body forward. Slide your left forearm into the back of his shoulder, dropping your weight against his shoulder and body for control. Release the grip with your right hand on his wrist, check his arm downward with your left hand, and throw a right punch to the head.

Knife Forward Grip: As your opponent grabs your

wrist, it might at first appear as though you cannot use the knife against him, since he is controlling your knife hand. However, you can still stay within the basic framework of the technique and use the knife to cut his wrist. Perform the same move you would empty-handed, twisting your hand under and to the outside of your opponent's hand, cutting his wrist in the process. Proceed with a left inward block to the back of his elbow to hyperextend his arm until he bends forward. Lower your weight against his shoulder and body. Check his arm downward with your left hand and stab to his head or throat.

Knife Reverse Grip: Perform the same move, twisting your hand under and to the outside of your opponent's hand, cutting his wrist in the process. Proceed with a left inward block to his elbow to hyperextend his arm until he bends forward. Lower your weight against his shoulder and body. Check his arm downward with your left hand and throw a right punch toward his head, aiming slightly to the side. This allows you to slash his neck or throat.

Right Lapel Grab

Empty-Hand: Let's look at another upper body grab; a left hand grab to your right lapel. Why would somebody grab you this way? He might want to control your movement in preparation for a strike, or pull you toward him. Your empty-hand defense might involve pinning his grabbing hand to your shoulder with your left hand, simultaneously striking with a right palm strike to the back of his elbow to hyperextend his arm. Now that you have his attention, you might strike downward with your right hand into the crook of his elbow to bring his upper body forward, simultaneously striking with a left outward *shuto* to the throat. Throw a right hammer fist strike to the left side of the jaw followed by a right outward *shuto* to the right side of the neck.

Knife Forward Grip: As opponent grabs your right lapel with his left hand, pin his hand to your shoulder as you did in the empty-hand variation. But instead of striking palm up to the back of his elbow to hyperextend his arm, stab to his armpit. Technically, the technique could end here, because you have taken a primary target and the attack is bound to do significant damage. However, in order to stay within the basic framework of the empty-hand defense, you will now circle your right arm over the top of his arm and drop your elbow into the crook of his elbow to bring his upper body forward, as you throw a left outward *shuto* to the throat. Retrieve your hand to point of origin to avoid an inadvertent cut to yourself. Then slash outward to the throat or side of neck as a transitory move, reverse the motion and slash inward to the left side of the neck (in the motion of the hammer fist strike), and finish with an outward slash to the right side of neck (in the motion of the outward *shuto*). You have now remained within the basic framework of the technique also when wielding the knife.

Knife Reverse Grip: Pin opponent's hand to your shoulder with your free hand, and slash his triceps with the knife. Circle your right arm over the top of his and drop your elbow into the crook of his elbow to bring his upper body forward (you can also stab straight down into his clavicle and heart, and end the fight, but this would violate the original pattern of the empty-hand technique), as you throw a left outward *shuto* to his throat. Retrieve your hand to point of origin to avoid an inadvertent cut to yourself. Then slash outward to the throat or side of the neck as a transitory move. Stab to the left side of the neck. Twist your hand to slash through the neck as a transitory move, and stab to the right side of the neck.

Lapel Grab Cross

Empty-Hand: Opponent grabs your left lapel with his left hand. This is a slightly crossed rather than straight lapel grab, which places you in position to strike the back of his elbow with a right inward block to hyperextend his arm and loosen the grip. Simultaneously, pin his hand to your shoulder with your left hand. Throw a right front kick low to his left shin to split his focus and give him two points of pain. Drop your right elbow into the crook of his left elbow to bring his upper body forward. Immediately strike with a right upward elbow to the jaw, followed by a right hammer fist down on his nose.

Knife Forward Grip: Pin opponent's left hand to your left shoulder and stab straight to his armpit. Technically, this should end the fight. Throw a right front kick to his left shin to split his focus. Drop your right elbow into the crook of his elbow to bring his upper body forward. Stab upward to his throat or neck, twist the knife to slash through the neck as a transitory move, and slash diagonally downward to the left side of the neck.

Knife Reverse Grip: Pin opponent's hand to your shoulder with your left hand, and use the sharp edge of the blade to strike behind his elbow in an inward block motion to hyperextend and damage his arm simultaneously. Alternatively, you can slash his triceps instead, or strike with the pommel directly to the elbow. Throw a right front kick to his left shin to split his focus. Bring your right arm over the top of his arm and, as you drop your elbow downward, simultaneously stab to the heart or clavicle, if you can reach it, or alternatively to the biceps. This should end the fight. Slash diagonally upward and outward across the throat (palm up). Reverse the motion and stab diagonally downward to the left side of the neck.

Right Shoulder Grab (variation one)

Empty-Hand: Opponent grabs your right shoulder with his left hand from the side. You could initiate a defense intended to release the grip, or you could pin his hand to your shoulder for control. Let's say that you have determined that releasing the grip would be appropriate. An empty-hand defense for this grab might involve a right outward *shuto* to the inside of opponent's arm near the wrist to get him to release the grip, followed by a right front kick to the groin. As his upper body comes forward, meet his momentum by throwing a right palm strike to the jaw.

Knife Forward Grip: As opponent grabs your right shoulder with his left hand from the side, turn toward him and slash his biceps, forearm, or wrist. Then throw a right front kick to the groin. As his upper body comes forward, stab straight to the throat.

Knife Reverse Grip: As opponent grabs your right shoulder with his left hand from the side, turn toward him and slash his biceps, forearm, or wrist. Then throw a right front kick to the groin. Punch toward the jaw with the hand holding the knife, but aim slightly to the side, allowing the blade to impact the target and slash the throat.

Right Shoulder Grab (variation two)

Empty-Hand: Opponent grabs your right shoulder with his left hand from the side. Pin his hand to your shoulder with your left hand, simultaneously striking with a right finger whip to the eyes. Bring your right elbow down into the crook of his elbow. As you drop your weight, his knees should bend, bringing his upper body down. Strike with a right upward *shuto* to the throat.

Knife Forward Grip: Pin opponent's hand to your shoulder with your left hand, simultaneously stabbing straight to the eyes. This requires turning your hand palm up. If you prefer to keep your hand palm down, an alternative is to slash outward from left to right across the face or neck. Technically, this should end the fight. However, to stay true to the empty-hand technique, you will now bring your right elbow down into the crook of his elbow as you drop your weight. As soon as his body drops forward, stab straight to his throat, or alternatively slash outward from left to right across his throat.

Knife Reverse Grip: Pin opponent's hand to your shoulder, simultaneously stabbing, palm down, to the eyes. Technically, this should end the fight. Bring your right elbow down into the crook of his elbow as you drop your weight. As soon as his body drops forward, stab upward to his throat, turning the palm of your hand to the outside in the reverse bow motion.

Side Waist Grab

Empty-Hand: Opponent grabs the right side of your belt with his left hand. You could certainly start this technique like you would the shoulder grab, by pinning his hand with your left hand to control his movement, and striking to the eyes with a finger whip. But let's try a different variation. For your empty-hand defense, pin his hand with your left hand and strike with a right back fist to his nose. Circle your arm behind his arm and against the back of his elbow to hyperextend his arm. Reverse the motion, striking with a right back fist to the midsection to bring his upper body forward. Grab the hair toward the back of his neck with your left hand to control him, and drop a right *shuto* down on the back of the neck.

Knife Forward Grip: Pin opponent's hand with your left hand and stab (palm up) to his throat, or alternatively, slash outward (palm down) from left to right across his throat. Technically, this should end the fight. Circle your arm behind his arm and against the back of his elbow to hyperextend his arm. Reverse the motion, slashing diagonally upward from left to right across the throat. Grab the hair toward the back of his neck with your left hand to control him, and stab downward to the back of the neck, or alternatively, turn your hand with the palm toward you and strike with the pommel to the back of the neck. As you can see, the technique requires some minor adjustments, but you will still stay within the basic framework of the original empty-hand technique.

Grip Reverse Grip: Pin opponent's hand with your left hand and stab upward to his throat in the reverse bow motion. Technically, this should end the fight. Circle your arm behind his arm and against the back of his elbow to hyperextend his arm. Reverse the motion and stab to the abdomen. Alternatively, upon stabbing upward to his throat, you could also forego circling your arm around his, and instead drop your hand and stab directly to his abdomen. As his body slumps forward, grab the hair toward the back of his neck with your left hand to control him, and stab downward in a hammer fist motion to the back of the neck.

Front Waist Grab

Empty-Hand: Opponent grabs you in a front waist grab with both hands on your belt. Your empty-hand defense calls for dropping your weight simultaneously to landing hammer fist strikes with your right and left hands to his wrists to break the grip. Throw two simultaneous uppercuts to the sides of his body (liver and spleen, or floating ribs). Cross your forearms, right over left, and throw an upward X-strike to the throat. Claw outward across the face with both hands simultaneously, and throw a right inward *shuto* to the left side of the neck.

Knife Forward Grip: As opponent grabs your belt, drop your weight and strike with both hands to his wrists, but angle your fists palm down in a slight outward motion. This allows you to slash his left wrist with the knife in your right hand. Be aware that you may risk cutting your left hand inadvertently, particularly if you have a long blade. When throwing the uppercuts, stab to the stomach or spleen. Technically, this should end the fight. Throw an upward X-strike to the throat, immediately upon contact pulling your arms outward so as to enact an outward slash with the knife across the front of the throat. Again, be careful so that you don't inadvertently slash your own wrist (this is always a danger when your arms are crossed). Slash to the left side of opponent's neck in the motion of an inward *shuto* from right to left.

Knife Reverse Grip: As opponent grabs your belt, drop your weight and strike with both hands to his wrists, stabbing with the knife in your right hand to his left forearm or wrist. This strike requires a bit of precision. Do not attempt to stab directly to his hand, as a tiny bit of misjudgment might cause you to stab yourself in the gut, hip, or thigh. You can also drop your hands to the inside of his arms, and then turn your knife hand palm up and slash outward from left to right across his forearm, or directly to his throat as you extend your arm. Throw the uppercuts to the midsection, slashing outward across the abdomen. Throw the upward X-strike to the throat and slash outward from left to right across the throat. Stab inward to the left side of the neck. Be aware that your hands are crossed on the X-strike, and be careful not to inadvertently cut your own wrist when uncrossing your forearms. Experiment with slight variations in order to avoid inadvertent injury to yourself, while staying within the basic framework of the technique.

Rear Choke

Empty-Hand: Opponent grabs you with both hands around the neck in a rear choke. Your empty-hand defense calls for turning to your right and striking the back of his right elbow with your right elbow to release the grip. Extend your arm and throw a right back fist to the temple, followed by a left palm strike to the jaw. Clear his arms downward and out of the way with your left hand. Throw a right upward elbow to the chin, and then drop a right hammer fist to the nose.

Knife Forward Grip: Turn toward opponent and strike with your right elbow to the back of his right elbow to release the grip. Instead of throwing a right back fist to the temple, turn your hand palm up and stab to the throat in the back fist motion. Then throw a left palm strike to the jaw. Clear his arms downward and out of the way with your left hand, and stab straight to his gut. This move substitutes for the upward elbow strike, while remaining within the motion of the same. This move should also end the fight.

Knife Reverse Grip: Turn toward opponent and strike with your right elbow to the back of his right elbow to release the grip. Turn your fist palm up and extend your arm in the back fist motion, slashing outward from left to right across the neck. Throw a left palm strike to the jaw. Clear his arms downward and out of the way with your left hand, and slash in the upward elbow motion diagonally and slightly outward to the neck. Stab straight down to the face, throat, or chest in the hammer fist motion, depending on how his body is positioned. As you can see, you have once again used the knife in both forward and reverse grip while staying within the basic framework of the empty-hand technique as originally designed.

Headlock

Empty-Hand: Opponent grabs you in a headlock, with his left arm around the back of your neck, clasping his hands at the front. Both your hands are free. Strike with a right hammer fist to the back of his neck, simultaneously striking with a left hammer fist to his groin. Grab his hair with your right hand and pull his head back, while pushing against the chin with your left hand to aid the movement. Release the grip on his hair and strike with a straight right punch to his left kidney.

Knife Forward Grip: When opponent grabs you in a headlock, strike with the pommel to the back of his neck, simultaneously striking his groin with a left hammer fist. Alternatively, turn your hand palm down, stabbing to the back of his neck, which should technically end the fight (the pommel strike might not). You cannot grab his hair with your right hand, because it requires letting go of the knife. Instead, as you push your left hand against the chin, stab to the left kidney.

Knife Reverse Grip: When opponent grabs you in a headlock, stab to the back of his neck or spine, simultaneously striking his groin with a left hammer fist. The knife provides you with a few inches greater reach, which may make it easier to reach your opponent's neck. You cannot grab his hair with your right hand, because it requires letting go of the knife. Instead, as you push your left hand against the chin, stab to the left kidney.

EMPTY-HAND AND KNIFE COMPARISONS IN PUNCH TECHNIQUE DEFENSES

We have now explored a few common grab technique defenses, and how these can be used when empty-handed or armed with a knife in forward and reverse grip. But what if your opponent throws a strike instead? Can you still apply the same defensive principles you use in your empty-hand martial art when armed with a knife? We will now look at a few ways to defend against strikes by positioning to the inside along the opponent's centerline, and to the outside away from his centerline or slightly toward his back. This is generally considered the superior position, because you eliminate or at least decrease his ability to use one or both hands against you. Although you don't have equal access to the primary targets along the centerline, such as the heart, solar plexus, midsection, and groin, there are still many good targets available from the outside position.

Straight Right Punch (inside variation)

Empty-Hand: Let's say your opponent throws a straight right strike, and your empty-hand defense calls for assuming a right fighting stance and defending with a right inward block to the inside of his forearm, followed by a right back fist to the temple, and a left outward *shuto* (palm down) to the throat. Technically, these strikes should end the fight, since you have prevented his strike from hitting you and countered with two strikes to primary targets. The back fist to the temple could easily knock him unconscious, and if not, the *shuto* to the throat could break the windpipe and definitely end the fight. But to be on the safe side, you continue with a right uppercut to the solar plexus. This should bring his upper body forward. You now throw another left outward *shuto* to the throat, a right hammer fist to the left side of the jaw, and a right outward *shuto* to the right side of the neck.

Knife Forward Grip: Now, let's implement the knife while staying true to the original pattern of the technique. With the knife in forward grip, block your opponent's strike with the edge of the blade to the inside of his forearm, or alternatively slash his wrist. You might strike with the pommel to the temple next, but you can also change the angle and targets slightly and within the same motion slash across the throat from left to right. Follow with the left outward *shuto* to the throat, as you pull the knife hand toward you and stab straight to the abdomen. Throw another left outward *shuto* to the throat, as you pull the knife out of the abdomen and slash diagonally inward to the left side of the neck and diagonally outward to the right side of the neck.

Knife Reverse Grip: Block with the edge of the blade to the inside of opponent's forearm, or alternatively slash his wrist. Then stab straight to the temple or side of neck. Follow with a left outward *shuto* to the throat. Be cautious so as to avoid an inadvertent cut to your own hand when you withdraw the knife and extend the *shuto*. Because of the reverse grip, the stab to the abdomen is no longer convenient (unless you choose to go into reverse bow), so you must alter the strike slightly. For instance, you might slash diagonally upward and outward to the throat, then throw another left outward *shuto* to the throat, and stab to the left side of the neck. Pull the knife back toward you, or alternatively twist it and slash through the neck and then stab to the right side of the neck.

Right Wide Looping Punch (inside variation)

Empty-Hand: Let's say your opponent throws a wide looping punch (a so-called haymaker) instead of a straight right. Haymakers lend themselves to working along your opponent's centerline. To defend against a haymaker thrown with the right hand, your empty-hand martial art calls for blocking the strike with your left forearm almost in the motion of a rising block, simultaneously stepping forward and at a slight angle to the right with your right foot to avoid the strike's path of power. As your lead foot plants, throw a vertical right strike to the ribs or midsection, then a low right sidekick to the left shin or knee, followed by a right downward hammer fist strike to the groin (reverse bow motion). As his upper body comes forward, throw a right horizontal elbow strike to the head.

Knife Forward Grip: Block the strike with your left forearm almost in the motion of a rising block, simultaneously stepping forward and to the right with your right foot. Stab to opponent's side below the ribcage. This strike should technically end the fight, but to be on the safe side, throw a low right sidekick to the left shin or knee. Strike with the pommel to the groin (reverse bow motion). As his upper body comes forward, stab to the left side of the neck in the motion of the horizontal elbow strike. If you find it awkward to transition from the pommel strike to the groin to the stab to the left side of the neck, you can add a transition strike, such as diagonal slash from left to right across the throat.

Knife Reverse Grip: Block the strike with your left forearm almost in the motion of a rising block, simultaneously stepping forward and to the right with your right foot. However, because of the reverse grip, the knife is not in position for a stab to the midsection under the ribcage. Try a slash from right to left across the midsection instead. Throw the low right sidekick to the left shin or knee, and stab to the groin (reverse bow motion). As his upper body comes forward, slash inward from right to left across the neck in the motion of the horizontal elbow strike. If you find it awkward to transition from the stab to the groin to the slash to the left side of the neck, you can add a transition strike, such as diagonal slash (palm up) from left to right across the throat.

Straight Right Punch (outside variation one)

Empty-Hand: Opponent throws a right strike. You will now be working toward his outside, slightly toward his back. Your empty-hand defense calls for assuming a left fighting stance. Parry the strike with your left (lead) hand to the back of opponent's elbow. Drop your weight and, using appropriate body rotation, throw a right reverse punch to the ribs. Circle the strike slightly toward you and reverse the motion, throwing a right outward *shuto* to the right kidney. Follow with a low right sidekick to the back of the right knee. As opponent's upper body comes back, slap his left ear with your left hand and throw a right horizontal elbow strike to the right side of his head.

Knife Forward Grip: From a left fighting stance, parry the strike with your left hand to the back of opponent's elbow. Drop your weight and stab straight to the soft tissue area below the ribs on the right side of his body. Technically, this should end the fight, but to stay true to the empty-hand technique, you will now twist the knife and slash from right to left through the soft tissue of the midsection, then reverse the motion and slash from left to right to the right kidney. Follow with a low right sidekick to the back of the right knee. As opponent goes down and his upper body comes back, slap his left ear with your left hand, and stab to the right side of the neck in the motion of the horizontal elbow strike.

Knife Reverse Grip: From a left fighting stance, parry the strike with your left hand to the back of opponent's elbow. Drop your weight and slash from right to left across the ribs under the arm. Reverse the motion and stab to the right kidney. Throw a low right sidekick to the back of the right knee. As opponent goes down and his upper body comes back, slap his left ear with your left hand, and slash the right side of the neck in the motion of the horizontal elbow strike.

Straight Right Punch (outside variation two)

Empty-Hand: Let's say your opponent throws a straight right strike, and your empty-hand defense calls for assuming a left fighting stance and parrying the strike downward with your left hand. Following the parry, step forward to a right fighting stance, simultaneously striking with a vertical punch to the nose. Check his arm downward with your right hand, then fold your arm and throw a right horizontal elbow to the face or side of head. Reverse the motion and throw a right outside *shuto* to the side or back of the neck.

Knife Forward Grip: From a left fighting stance, parry the strike downward with your left hand. Step forward to a right fighting stance, simultaneously stabbing straight to opponent's throat. Check his arm downward with the pommel, then fold your arm and stab to left the side of the neck in the motion of the horizontal elbow strike. Twist the knife and slash through the neck, and stab to the right side of the neck.

Knife Reverse Grip: From a left fighting stance, parry the strike downward with your left hand. Step forward to a right fighting stance, simultaneously slashing opponent's arm from wrist to biceps. Make sure you have retrieved your parrying hand first in order to avoid an inadvertent cut to your own hand. Strike with the pommel to the nose. Stab downward to the clavicle. Retrieve the knife and slash from right to left across the throat in the motion of the horizontal elbow strike. Reverse motion and stab to the right side of the neck.

Straight Left Punch (outside variation)

Empty-Hand: As opponent throws a left strike, your empty-hand defense calls for assuming a right fighting stance and stepping slightly forward and to the right to remain to the outside of the strike. Block the strike with a double parry (right/left) to the outside of opponent's arm. Continue the circular motion of your hands and throw a right inward *shuto* to the back of the neck and a left vertical punch to the ribs. Drop your weight slightly and throw a left horizontal elbow strike to the ribs. Reverse the motion and throw a left outward *shuto* to the left kidney, followed by a right inward *shuto* to the right kidney.

Knife Forward Grip: From a right fighting stance, step slightly forward and to the right and slash the back of opponent's wrist, hand, or fingers. Check his arm with the back of your left hand in the motion of the double parry. A note of caution: Since the double parry requires your arms or hands to cross each other's path momentarily, you must be particularly aware when wielding a knife, in order to avoid cutting your own hand. Make each move distinct. Thus, when you have slashed your opponent's wrist, hand, or fingers, bring your knife hand back to point of origin before executing the outward parry with your left hand. Now, either stab to the back of opponent's neck (upper spine), or slash inward from right to left across the side of his neck. Technically, this should end the fight. But to eliminate further potential danger, while staying true to the empty-hand technique, throw a left vertical punch to the ribs under his arm, followed by a left horizontal elbow strike to the ribs as you drop your weight slightly. Reverse the motion and throw a left outward *shuto* to the left kidney, followed by a slash to the right kidney.

Knife Reverse Grip: From a right fighting stance, step slightly forward and to the right and slash opponent's wrist, hand, or fingers. Retrieve your hand to point of origin to avoid slashing your own hand or arm, and execute an outward parry with your left hand. Continue the motion of your right hand and stab to the back of opponent's neck, or alternatively slash from right to left across the side of the neck. Technically, this should end the fight, but to be on the safe side and stay within the perimeters of the empty-hand technique, follow with a left vertical punch to the ribs under his arm, and a left horizontal elbow strike to the ribs as you drop your weight slightly. Reverse the motion and throw a left outward *shuto* to the left kidney, followed by stab to the right kidney.

Right-Left Combination (inside variation)

Empty-Hand: Opponent throws a straight right punch followed by a straight left punch. Your empty-hand defense calls for assuming a right fighting stance and a right inward block to the inside of opponent's right forearm, followed by a right outward block (palm forward) to the inside of the left forearm. Next, throw a left outward *shuto* to the throat. This will technically end the fight, but to be on the safe side, throw a right uppercut to the solar plexus to bring his upper body forward, followed by a right diagonal downward elbow strike to the head.

Knife Forward Grip: Block to the inside of opponent's right forearm, or alternatively slash his wrist. Turn your hand palm out and block or slash to the inside of the left forearm or wrist. Alternatively, you can also slash the throat in the transitory move from one block to the next, by extending your arm slightly. Should you prove successful at slashing the throat, the fight would end here. Otherwise, throw a left outward *shuto* to the throat, followed by a stab to the abdomen, followed by a stab to the left side of the neck within the motion of an elbow strike.

Knife Reverse Grip: Block or slash to the inside of opponent's right forearm or wrist. Turn your hand palm out and block or slash to the inside of his left forearm or wrist. Throw a left outward *shuto* to the throat. Strike with the pommel in the uppercut motion to the midsection, and as his body comes forward, slash upward and outward from left to right across the throat. Then slash inward and downward to the left side of the neck in the motion of an elbow strike.

EMPTY-HAND AND KNIFE COMPARISONS IN FORMS PRACTICE

Now that we have looked at how to practice basic stances, blocks, strikes, and kicks with the knife, and learned how to implement the knife in empty-handed grab and punch techniques, most traditional stand-up martial arts also teach forms (or kata). These are series of individual moves strung together into techniques, which are then strung together into a continuous pattern that is performed against an imaginary opponent. A problem with forms practice is that it could easily become mundane, with the same sequence of techniques practiced in a single fluid pattern every time. Since there is no real opponent, much of the unpredictability inherent to fighting and self-defense is lost. As a result, the form can easily become a mindless rut; in other words, a set of moves that have little meaning. When you pick up the knife, the moves in the form will take on new meaning, as you rethink how each move should be executed for greatest effect, while remaining aware of your imaginary opponent's possible defenses and other dangers that occur as a result of wielding a knife.

First, be attentive to your stance. Is it rigid, or do you use body rotation when striking? How do you hold your guard (your hands)? Sometimes, tradition doesn't allow us to change the form. But experimenting with the width of your stance, increased or decreased body rotation, and positioning your guard the way you would in sparring, might benefit you when applying what you have learned in the form to empty-handed or armed knife combat.

That said, martial arts forms are composed of many moves that can be used for a variety of purposes. A punch, block, or pressure point strike may essentially utilize the same body mechanics. Which particular technique (punch, block, pressure point strike) is "intended" in the form depends on what the practitioner visualizes. If you have learned blocks, this is probably the application you will see when practicing the form. If you have learned pressure point strikes, then this is probably what you will see. Now, pick up a practice knife (or two knives, one in each hand) and run through a basic form from your empty-hand martial art. If a move in your form calls for a block with your right hand followed by a block with your left hand, you might slash with the knife in your right hand and cover or parry with your left hand, without changing the basic pattern of the form.

Many forms also involve both hands equally. This is thus an opportunity to practice forms with a knife in your dominant hand (your right hand if you are right-handed); with a knife in your non-dominant hand; or with a knife in each hand. You can also practice with single- and double-edged knives and note any necessary adjustments. The single-edged knife in particular requires awareness of the direction of the cutting edge, to ensure that it always faces your imaginary adversary and never yourself. You can also practice with one knife in forward and the other in reverse grip, and explore how to stay true to the original empty-hand form. If your martial art teaches other weapons forms, such as short sticks, long staff, sword, sai, or nunchaku, practice sessions can be made even more interesting if you substitute these weapons for knives. How would you do a long staff form, putting the staff aside and picking up two knives, one in each hand, for example? How would you practice the nunchaku techniques with knives in your hands instead of nunchakus? As you can see, there is a lot you can do with forms practice once you start implementing knives.

Let's say that a technique in one of your forms involves the following empty-hand moves:

1. Step forward with your right foot to a right fighting stance as you inward block your opponent's strike with your right hand. Your left hand stays high, guarding your head against counterstrikes.

2. Strike with a right outward *shuto* to the throat.

3. Throw a left horizontal spear hand (palm down) to the eyes.

4. Throw a right vertical spear hand (palm left) to the soft tissue under the ribs.

Now, pick up a knife in your right hand, forward grip. Go through the techniques in the form again, blocking the strike by slashing opponent's wrist as you step forward to a right fighting stance. Immediately extend the knife and slash across the throat from left to right. Your left hand technique remains the same as in the empty-hand version of the form, with a left horizontal spear to the eyes. Then stab to the soft tissue under the ribs.

Now, do the same technique again with the knife in reverse grip. Step forward to a right fighting stance, blocking to the inside of opponent's forearm or slashing his wrist, then stabbing straight to the throat. Your left hand technique remains the same as in the empty-hand version, with a left horizontal spear to the eyes. You must now make a small adjustment because, due to the reverse grip, you don't have a stab available to the soft tissue under the ribs. What can be done? You might change the technique slightly and slash outward from left to right across the midsection instead.

Now, pick up two knives, one in each hand, and hold both knives in forward grip. The only thing that changes is the left spear to the eyes, which will now be a straight stab to the eyes. Switch both knives to reverse grip. Again, the only thing that changes is the left spear to the eyes, which will now be a slash across the face or throat due to the reverse grip, or alternatively a strike with the pommel to the jaw or temple.

Do the exercise once more with one knife in forward grip and the other in reverse grip and note the targets and minor required changes. As you can see, even a simple four-move technique can be quite interesting once you pick up one or two knives and start experimenting with different grips. There is a whole lot more to the technique than first meets the eyes, and proficiency requires forethought and experimentation. Good luck with your continued training!

Knife Training and Advanced Martial Arts Concepts

Book 10

Knife Training Methods and Techniques for Martial Artists

by Martina Sprague

TABLE OF CONTENTS

Introduction	273
Brief History	276
Lesson Objectives	278
Mechanical vs. Conceptual Learning	279
What to Look For	287
Time and Timing	294
Speed	299
Pressing the Attack	302
Distance and Positioning	305
Movement and Footwork	308
Disarming the Opponent or Not?	311
Furthering the Learning Experience	317
Something to Think About for Future Training	323

INTRODUCTION

Now that we have explored how knife and empty-hand techniques compare in Book 9 of the *Knife Training Methods and Techniques for Martial Artists* series, we should look at how to apply concepts rather than the specific techniques from your empty-hand martial art when armed with a knife or defending against a knife attack. What is a concept? A concept is an idea, or the underlying current that drives a technique. For example, distance control is a concept that includes your zone of safety where your opponent cannot reach you, and often where you cannot reach him. When in this zone, you may still have the option of flight, because the confrontation, although imminent, has not yet developed to the physical stage. The safety zone is also the distance where your senses are heightened in preparation for a physical confrontation. When in the safety zone, you can size up your opponent and attempt to determine his motives and whether or not he has a weapon.

In empty-hand martial arts, distance and the safety zone relate to preparing your body for blocking a possible attack, or kicking to keep an advancing attacker away or taking him out entirely, for example, with a head or leg kick that drops him to the ground. Or you might preempt the attack through a quick move forward. Yet an option is to lure him to come toward you at a suitable time that allows you to pursue an offensive or defensive technique that renders him harmless.

As opposed to a gun encounter, for instance, which works better from medium to long range, because of the nature of empty-hand martial arts, you can only use your skills when within reach of your adversary, or from close range. Having possession of a knife when faced with an unarmed aggressor gives you an advantage in reach, as long as you deploy your weapon in time and are mentally prepared to use it. Distance, range, and position concepts that apply to your empty-hand martial art and that are transferable to knife fighting also include superior positioning toward your opponent's back or weak side, where he cannot reach you or does not have the flexibility to use his hands or kicks against you, and fighting from trapping range where pinning or trapping an arm eliminates most of your adversary's movement. Other valuable martial arts concepts that apply to knife training include speed and determination (being first wins), and keeping your strikes within the confines of your body to increase speed, avoid wasted motion, and protect your openings.

As you proceed, remember that learning about the knife in the martial arts often involves a setting where you are expected to defend against a bladed weapon empty-handed. But, as stressed repeatedly throughout the *Knife Training Methods and Techniques for Martial Artists* series, all fighting involves two parts: offense and defense. Although our ultimate goal is to protect against danger, proficiency in offense with the knife will aid proficiency also in defense. Although martial arts schools tend to teach strictly technique, a well-versed martial artist must spend considerable time practicing concepts involving timing, coordination, ease of movement, and fighter mentality.

As explained in Book 1, the *Knife Training Methods and Techniques for Martial Artists* series has three objectives: The first few books focus on getting to know the knife, its strengths and weaknesses, and on manipulating and using it. The next few books focus on defending against knife attacks. The last few books focus on implementing empty-hand martial arts skills into your knife training, and include scenario-based exercises intended to bring your knowledge into perspective and give you a solid understanding of your strengths and weaknesses when faced with a knife-wielding assailant. Each book starts with an introduction. You are then given the lesson objectives, along with detailed information and a number of training exercises aimed at making you physically and emotionally ready to participate in traditional martial arts demonstrations involving a knife or, if fate will have it, in a real encounter. Remember that it is your responsibility to know and comply with all federal and local laws regarding the possession and carry of edged weapons.

BRIEF HISTORY

Why train with the knife when you're already proficient at empty-hand skills? Because weapon training heightens our respect for the martial arts, broadens our views, and increases our skills and insights. It teaches us that, when armed with a weapon, we must be in charge of the confrontation. You literally hold the key to life and death in your hand. This power requires deep contemplation and the understanding that you should not take your skills lightly or be careless with your martial art.

How we think about and debate the usefulness of edged weapons has not changed much through history. For example, the opinions of the various European medieval sword masters as to the "best" type of combat sword or fencing weapon varied widely.

Historical Gem: As with most martial disciplines, disagreement existed among the scholars of swordsmanship. Some held the view that a cut constituting "a hard, fast strike with the edge of the weapon that may then be drawn or pushed to increase the damage" was best, and should therefore be the most frequently used method of attack. See Guy Windsor, *The Swordsman's Companion* (Highland Village, TX: The Chivalry Bookshelf, 2004), 82. Italian fencing master Giacomo Di Grassi, in *His True Art of Defence*, furthered this idea by arguing that the edge proved superior to the point, particularly if the opponent had parried the initial thrust and the sword was no longer in position to be thrust a second time. See Giacomo Di Grassi, *His True Art of Defence*, adapted by William Elder (London, UK:

1594). Others argued that the long handle benefited the swordsman when using the sword primarily as a thrusting weapon. A thrust with the point through vulnerable targets not protected by armor, such as the armpit, could prove deadly particularly if the sword penetrated the vital organs.

The swordsmen of medieval Europe thus used every part of the sword—the blade, the hilt, the pommel—in attack and defense. It mattered less whether one used fancy or crude techniques, whether one slashed or thrust with the sword. The end result, the death or undisputed defeat of the opponent, remained the same.

LESSON OBJECTIVES

Upon completion of this lesson, you should:

1. Have gained an understanding of how to move from the mechanical to the conceptual stage of learning, and why this progress is necessary for learning successful defenses against knife attacks

2. Have studied how fights are likely to start and how you might react to a perceived threat that has not yet developed into a physical battle

3. Have explored how to take advantage of different kinds of timing, and developed an understanding of the relationship between time and timing

4. Have experimented with factors that trigger the natural speed of your body, and how best to use your empty hand along with your knife to end the fight as quickly as possible

5. Have developed an understanding of the importance of seizing the initiative, and why pressing the attack will benefit you more often than not

6. Have thought about and experimented with your safety zone, and how distance, movement, and footwork can prove elusive

7. Have practiced different ways to disarm your opponent of his weapon, and different ways to disable the use of his weapon without disarming him

MECHANICAL VS. CONCEPTUAL LEARNING

We will start this book with a short discussion of how we normally progress from the beginning to advanced stages of learning, and why we must eventually leave the mechanical stage and move to the conceptual stage to get the most out of our empty-hand martial art and knife training.

Mechanical learning, also called rote, is the first stage of learning and is necessary to know how to perform a defensive technique with precision and confidence. But once you have learned how to do the technique mechanically, in order to become proficient to the point that you can rely on it in a true self-defense encounter, you must go beyond the mechanical stage. Now that you have studied knife offense and defense in various forms, as taught in previous books of the *Knife Training Methods and Techniques for Martial Artists* series, to enhance your experience even more, or to demonstrate and teach the material to others with confidence, start by examining the stages of each technique and identifying matters of importance. For example:

1. Explain and demonstrate the mechanics of a defensive slash to your opponent's arm. This can initially be done against a stationary and cooperative partner. Identify the best part of the arm for the attack; for instance, the wrist or fingers in order to disable his ability to continue the attack, especially if he is armed with an edged weapon.

2. Expand on the technique by identifying targets for your follow-up move. As learned in previous books of the

Knife Training Methods and Techniques for Martial Artist series, after taking a secondary target (target taken as initial defense against an attack, such as the arm or hand), attempt a stab or slash to a primary target (target taken with the intent of ending the fight, such as the throat or midsection).

3. Examine how to adapt when your opponent approaches you from different angles. We know by now that defending successfully against a knife attack done with intent is not a simple matter of attacking a secondary followed by a primary target. Once movement and unpredictability is added to the attack, good timing becomes crucial to success.

4. Identify the dangers associated with the technique. Might it result in balance loss or target exposure? Should you avoid the attack initially; for example, by retreating in the hope that the attack will miss, and then advancing while your opponent recovers? Or is it better to time your defense to the initiation of his technique, or even preempt it?

When you have chosen, practiced, and demonstrated a few common defenses that seem suitable to your particular martial art, with time you will start associating specific techniques with specific scenarios. You will begin to see opportunities for using these techniques. The idea is to take you back to a point of familiarity, where you can sense the value of a specific technique without having to dwell on it. For instance, every time your practice partner attacks with an inward slash, you know that if you can time your empty-hand defense properly by moving inside of the attack and blocking his arm, you can immediately follow with a palm strike to the jaw, for example, and then control the attacking arm and weapon by taking your opponent to the ground with an unbalancing move. If armed with a knife, you might likewise move inside of the attack, simultaneously slashing your opponent's wrist or knife hand and follow with a slash to the throat or straight stab to the abdomen. In both scenarios, you should recognize that your initial move calls for moving to close range inside of the attack. This is true whether he attacks with his right or left hand. If the angle of attack changes slightly; for example, if he attacks with an overhead downward stab instead of an inward swing, you can essentially rely on the same principles, moving inside of the attack and simultaneously blocking his arm on its downward motion.

Every time your opponent attacks with an inward slash or stab, you might see an opportunity for blocking to the inside of his arm and attacking with a finishing strike to his face or throat. Practice the defense empty-handed at first, and then with the knife. Your empty-hand technique might be done as demonstrated in the picture. When practicing with the knife, you might slash your opponent's wrist first or, as an alternative, do the same block as you did empty-handed, and simultaneously stab to his throat. Image source: Martina Sprague.

Attacking different targets than initially learned, or reversing the pattern of a technique, will also move you away from the mechanical stage, but requires some forethought or retraining. When engaging in this type of exercise, techniques will begin to mean more. For example, a defense against an inward slash in a knife-on-knife scenario might call for blocking the attack by slashing your opponent's wrist, immediately followed by slash to his throat. You might reverse the order of these two moves, for example, by preempting the attack. Start with a slash to the throat, and then slash the wrist to disarm the adversary. The danger is obviously that your opponent still has access to his knife when you take the primary target, and you must move inside of his effective range in order to execute this technique successfully. The objective, however, is to learn to bypass the secondary target (his wrist or hand) and go directly for the primary target (his throat) when you recognize an opportunity for preempting the attack, perhaps before he has fully deployed his weapon. While your goal is ultimately to get past the mechanical stage and to the understanding, application, and correlation stages of learning, you might want to learn a reasonable amount of detail about the technique before practicing it in reverse or implementing different concepts.

Many empty-hand martial arts techniques involve several strikes to different targets. The whole technique may comprise twenty individual moves. Not only is it time consuming to learn self-defense this way, if events don't go as expected you might get confused somewhere in the middle of the technique and halt or delay your defense or counterattack. We also often assume that the assailant will remain stationary and not retaliate while we complete the moves. A good approach to learning self-defense may be to learn a few highly effective techniques that instantly steal your opponent's balance or place him or her in an inferior position. Identify techniques that are easy to learn, and that the average person can apply with a reasonable amount of training. Now explore how these techniques can be used also against a person armed with a knife. Does the manner of his attack matter? If the technique is effective against an inward slash with the knife in forward grip, is it still as effective against a straight stab, a downward stab with the knife in the ice pick grip, or several quick slashes with the knife in reverse grip? A technique that works well as defense against an empty-handed assailant may or may not work as well when he is armed with a knife.

Many empty-hand martial arts also teach a multitude of techniques as defenses against a multitude of attacks. Although this type of learning can prove stimulating, it also complicates the ability to respond spontaneously to an attack. To speed up the learning process, when implementing the knife in your empty-hand training, rely on techniques that you already know and have committed to muscle memory. This is better than learning a whole new set of techniques particularly designed for the knife. But it requires an ability to think in somewhat abstract terms and apply slight variations of a technique within its original pattern. The best way to gain proficiency with the knife quickly is to find movement patterns that are easy to perform for the natural workings of your body; in other words, movement patterns that don't seem contradictory to your anatomy and body mechanics, or that are needlessly complicated.

There are several other ways to move from the mechanical to the conceptual stage of learning. For example, rather than thinking technique, think direction; rather than thinking front kick or inward *shuto* (also called knife-hand strike) in empty-hand martial arts, think which path these strikes follow (straight for the front kick, and inward curve for the *shuto*), and vary the technique slightly depending on the distance to your target. A front kick can be thrown with the shin to the groin from mid-range, or with the knee from close range. A *shuto* can be converted to a hook at mid-range, or an elbow strike at close range while still following the same basic pattern. If you hold a knife in your hand, particularly in reverse grip, the hook can be made so tight that your fist misses the target, but the knife reaches the target, slashing your opponent's throat. The idea is to learn essentially the same body mechanics for each technique, until it becomes second nature and therefore spontaneous. Properly thrown, the *shuto*, hook, and elbow strike all employ the same motion, even though the striking weapon differs. A particular technique may not work from any range, but the particular motion of the technique may still work also when you hold a knife in your hand.

Now, take any technique from your empty-hand martial art and apply the same moves as defense against any type of attack. For example, the same moves with slight variations in height or angle that you use as defense against a wrist grab, can be used as defense against a myriad of scenarios. If the technique calls for a strike to your opponent's forearm or wrist, intended to break the grip, the same strike can also be used to his arm or wrist when he grabs you by the shoulder. Now, with the knife in your right hand, slash to your opponent's forearm whether attempting to break a grip on your wrist or defend against a strike to your head. Or slash to his neck as a preemptive move before he has the opportunity to grab you. The same motion is used in all three examples with only a slight variation in distance (how much you extend your arm), height, and angle.

Using the knife in defense and offense is not that complicated. But the more choices you have, the more hesitant you will become. If your arsenal includes only one strike and one target, there is no question which strike and target you will use. You can therefore respond immediately without stuttering to consider your options. If you have little time to train, learn some simple moves that will defend against your opponent's attack, followed by a couple of simple counterstrikes to primary targets; for example, a block to his arm followed by a slash across his neck and a stab to his midsection. The slash across the neck will technically end the fight, but should he have good reflexes and move out of the way, for instance, then the stab to the midsection will end the fight.

Eliminating or at least decreasing the uncertainty that often accompanies a fight or self-defense situation makes you stronger. Knowing what to do in advance is better than trying to adapt to a situation as it unfolds before you. Therefore, if you can use the knife in the empty-hand techniques you are already familiar with, you can gain confidence and proficiency faster.

WHAT TO LOOK FOR

Training in realistic self-defense teaches you about your limitations (perceived or otherwise). If you have an opportunity to attend a self-defense seminar that focuses on the knife, or sit in on a class at a knife- or weapon-training school, to get the most out of the event, you should come prepared and know what to focus on beforehand. Consider the following ideas prior to and after attending the event:

1. Identify how a fight starts, including body language, pointing, name calling, etc.

2. How capable are you of coping with a great deal of stress, such as you would experience when your life is threatened with an edged weapon? How much physical and mental training have you received prior to attending the seminar or event?

3. If you have a weapon available, or something that can be used as a weapon, your self-defense capability depends to some extent on your ability and readiness to use the weapon. Many self-defense seminars focus exclusively on defending empty-handed against a weapon attack, but there may also be many objects commonly found in the environment that can come to your assistance. When walking in the areas you tend to frequent often, pay attention to your surroundings and identify objects that you can easily reach and use as a shield or weapon of offense against a knife-wielding assailant.

4. If confined to your home when the attack happens, what types of objects can you find in your home that you can use as defense against a knife? You might think of the obvious, such as knives from your kitchen or other hard objects such as a broom handle for reach or a shoe as a striking weapon. But what about soft objects, such as a towel from the bathroom? A towel when wrapped around your arm can give you a great deal of protection against a bladed weapon, and allow you to move to close range where you can use your empty-hand martial arts skills.

5. If your assailant appears to be unarmed but suddenly deploys a knife, how will it change your reaction to the assault? You might at first have felt that you had the upper hand through years of martial arts training. But if all of this training has been empty-hand against empty-hand, when you realize your opponent is armed with a bladed weapon, can you still use your empty-hand skills with confidence, or will you freeze and be unable to act in this critical situation?

6. If you are in the process of defending against a knife attack when you lose your balance, and your opponent starts wrestling you on the ground, how might you defend yourself with his weight on top of you? To a person with no knife training, a stab would probably seem like the most basic technique, or even multiple stabs, particularly from the ice pick grip if in a wrestling match on the ground. If you are attending a self-defense seminar that includes knife defense, ask how you might defend against such an attack.

7. Consider threats that are confined to a specific area (like a room, stairwell, or parking garage), and how to maneuver toward the door or other escape route. How would you implement your empty-hand martial arts skills while attempting to reach the escape route?

Unless you are highly skilled at ground fighting, losing your balance and ending up on your back places you in an extremely inferior position. Experiment with a partner how you might defend yourself in a situation as pictured. Remember that falling on concrete is likely to knock the wind out of you at best and cause unconsciousness followed by death at worst. Image source: Martina Sprague.

When learning to defend against knife attacks, don't limit your studies to the physical aspects of the confrontation. Study also the underlying reasons behind the attack. For example, did it escalate from a verbal confrontation to a push or a punch, to a full-out brawl, and finally to the knife attack? Why would you or someone else get into a verbal confrontation in the first place, with the potential that it will escalate to a knife scenario? How might you end the confrontation while it is still at the verbal stage? Consider the fact that all attacks don't start verbally. If the assailant wants to rob you, he or she might attack without any prior warning.

Identify how a fight is likely to start. For example, does it start with name calling, followed by a push? At what point will you likely know that your opponent has a knife and is intending to use it against you? If you are carrying a knife, when would it be appropriate to deploy it? Image source: Martina Sprague.

It also helps to have an idea how to cause injury without causing death. In a self-defense situation, it is really your safety you are concerned with, and not whether your opponent lives or dies. In other words, if you can use your knife to instill a threat that is severe enough to deter the fight, or to injure your opponent enough to take away his will to fight, you might both walk away alive. When training with the knife, don't train with death as your primary goal. Even if you use the knife offensively, your goal is to bring yourself to safety. If this can be achieved without killing your opponent, or even without injuring him, you have reached one of the higher stages of martial arts study.

Historical Gem: Aikido was developed based on the premise that it is a strictly defensive art, using neither strikes nor kicks to counter an opponent's attack. Like other defensive martial arts, aikido has a negative aim: to avoid the aggressor's purpose. But unlike many other defensive arts, it has no positive aim of destroying the enemy forces. The hope is that the aggressor will realize the folly of his ways and pursue a path to peace instead. Although aikido falls in the category of "soft" arts, many martial arts in Asia were developed to break bones, kill the adversary, and end the fight as quickly as possible. They were not about humiliating the opponent by teaching him a lesson while letting him walk away physically unscathed.

A difference between empty-hand and knife techniques, and which has been noted repeatedly throughout the *Knife Training Methods and Techniques for Martial Artists* series of books, is that, whereas a strike with an empty fist must be straight and powerful, preferably with the weight of the body in coordinated motion behind it, a stab or slash with the knife can prove successful also if the weapon only glances the target, or if no bodyweight or hip rotation accompanies the strike.

Now try this simple defense for blocking and counterstriking with the knife. The X-block (crossing your forearms to block an attack) can be done upward or downward to defend against an overhead stab or an underhand or straight stab. Just as you would not stand straight in front of an adversary when blocking his empty-hand strike, you should be particularly cautious when he is wielding a knife. If the attack is an overhead strike with the weapon descending on you, it will probably have quite a bit of momentum behind it. It is therefore crucial that you sidestep the attack and block from an angle. You can block with your forearms against his, while holding the knife in your strong hand. As soon as the block is successful, slash with the knife to his wrist or up his arm and into his armpit, depending on the manner of his attack and in which hand you are holding the knife.

If using a downward X-block, for example, to block a front kick in empty-hand martial arts, or a straight punch or knife stab, again sidestep the attack to ensure that you don't meet power with power. You can then slash diagonally upward to the opponent's neck, or slash the Achilles tendon in his foot, if he is barefoot. These techniques work with the knife in forward grip.

Now, when switching to reverse grip and X-blocking an overhead attack, you can follow the block with a stab to the opponent's neck, or turn your hand palm up and slash in an outward motion to his neck or wrist if your knife hand is closer to this target. If X-blocking a straight stab with the knife in reverse grip, an outward stab to opponent's midsection or throat would work well following the block. You can also use an outward slash, if you turn your hand palm up.

A point of caution: When armed with a knife, and if your empty-hand martial art relies on crossing your arms to protect your centerline; for example, as when alternating inward and outward blocks, or as in a double parry, you may risk inadvertently cutting your own arm with the knife. Similarly, if your opponent throws a strike that you block with the knife in reverse grip and check his arm with your free hand, before slashing along his arm toward his throat, you may inadvertently cut your free left hand in the process, since it is in the path of the motion of the knife. While this move might work great with both hands empty, it could prove dangerous when armed with a knife. If you still want to use the left check to your opponent's arm, make sure that it is done in the fashion of a strike or quick push. Do not leave your hand in extended contact with his arm, but bring it back to point of origin quickly to prevent crossing the cutting edge of the knife over your own hand and arm.

TIME AND TIMING

Since the martial arts are unregulated, we will find many levels of skill among our black belt population. The martial artist, student and instructor alike, must therefore examine how realistic his or her training has been. You must also look at which types of techniques fit your mental inclination. Simply put, what types of moves do you like and where do you feel most comfortable? Which techniques have you trained in the most? Are you flexible enough to perform these techniques with balance, speed, and accuracy? Even a highly skilled individual may not want to rely on punching and kicking a heavier opponent into submission, because his smaller build will simply not produce the momentum needed to end a fight. This might be particularly crucial if you are defending empty-handed against a knife-wielding opponent. Consider that a person attacking you has probably some experience with street violence, and one strike or a little pain is not likely to stop him. If your first strike fails to end the fight, what will you do next?

When training for a street scenario, it is particularly important to consider realistic time. If a kick designed to stall a knife-wielding opponent's advance doesn't deter him, do you have enough time to try again before he is upon you? It might only take one stab or slash with the knife to end the fight. If going empty-handed against a knife-wielding adversary, the techniques you use must have a good chance of disarming him or controlling his weapon before he cuts you, preferably taking his balance, or at the very least forcing him to spend time to recover, time that you can use to distance yourself from the situation and get to safety. Many of the defenses and disarming techniques taught in the martial arts or practiced in the training hall are much too slow and complex for real time. When somebody intent on killing you attacks with a knife, he is not likely to halt his attack in midair and let you do an upward block followed by a complicated joint lock. When somebody rushes you from a distance of twenty feet, swinging his knife wildly, do you really have the physical capacity and presence of mind to halt his attack and subdue him? We would hope so, if you have spent some time learning about and practicing knife offense and defense. But theory cannot take the place of practice in real time.

If your opponent is going berserk, you must protect your vital targets, such as your neck. Practice with a partner to determine if you have what it takes to stop this type of attacker. Image source (slightly adapted): Sgt. Matthew Nedved, reproduced under Wikimedia Commons license.

Good martial arts practice should give you insight into your abilities and limitations. It is good to be confident, but it is not good to be overly confident. When we train in a known environment, we tend to fall into a rut; we train with the same people all the time, and we do the same techniques over and over according to specific patterns. As a result, we become complacent. When we train with people we know, we seldom use realistic force or realistic time. It is therefore difficult to determine whether or not your techniques really work the way they are designed. One of the best things you can do at this level of training is to shorten your defenses to simple moves while still retaining their effectiveness. A block followed by a palm strike to the jaw is better than an attempt to grab your opponent's knife hand while in motion, followed by a complex joint lock.

What type of person are you likely to encounter when training for the street rather than for competition or exercise, and what might be the manner of his attack? Do you reasonably believe that you will need to defend against a spinning back kick or a ridge hand strike, for example? Although these techniques are powerful, they only work for people schooled in karate. Is it reasonable to believe that your opponent will fight using traditional karate moves on the street? Street attacks may not be "clean." Your opponent will not throw one straight punch that you can sidestep or block. He will not swing at you with a knife exposed from several feet away.

A strike on the street is not necessarily a "clean" punch. It is therefore difficult to execute a "clean" block, or to sidestep the strike and avoid getting hurt. The same is true with a knife attack. You might have practiced defenses against straight stabs or wide slashes at a reasonable speed in the training hall. How skilled are you at defending against an attack at full speed, when you don't know in advance if it will be a stab or a slash with the knife in forward or reverse grip? Image source: Martina Sprague.

Consider your habits and past experiences when learning self-defense techniques against knife attacks. Carefully select the most effective techniques for the amount of time you have available. For example:

1. Evaluate the effectiveness of each technique you learn based on how intent the attacker is. If a technique

employs several strikes prior to a disarming attempt, you may only have time for one of these strikes before the assailant stabs or slashes you.

2. Learn how to finish the fight. We sometimes tend to block an attack or even block and counterstrike and then pause to see what happens. Push yourself to stay a step ahead of the assailant at all times. Press the attack (or your defense to the attack), so that you never give him the chance to recover and stab or slash you with the knife.

End the fight in the quickest way possible. Knife fighting techniques are not supposed to look fancy or pretty; they are supposed to be effective at ending the fight right now. The faster you strike a primary target, the greater is your economy of motion and the faster the fight will end. For example, when defending against a strike, attempted grab, or weapon attack, you might start by blocking the attack with the blade of the knife and then slashing your opponent's throat. This technique involves a two-count and will end the fight relatively quickly. But if your timing is really good, you might step inside of the technique, block the strike with your arm and simultaneously slash your opponent's throat. You have now reduced the time to a one-count. Explore the techniques in your empty-hand martial art to see if you can find suitable ways to cut out a step or two, and reach the primary target faster than what the technique initially calls for. Now explore these same techniques when armed with a knife.

SPEED

How can you improve the speed of your techniques? If your empty-hand martial art relies on circular moves, consider making the circle as small as possible when wielding the knife. A strike that travels through a large circle must cover a long distance. Although this might be great for a spinning heel kick, for example, because the kick can build a great deal of momentum by traveling through a longer distance, and therefore great power that will lead to great damage upon impact with the target, the knife is a touch weapon that doesn't need a lot of power to prove effective. If attacking with a slash, there is no need to swing the weapon excessively wide. A tiny circle on impact with the target is enough to slash through tissue.

As discussed previously, it is unrealistic to believe that you will be fast enough and have the precision to grab a strike that is thrown at you with full speed. However, blocking a strike is not as difficult as catching and grabbing. When attempting to grab, you should therefore block first to stall your opponent's momentum and freeze his motion for a fraction of a second. Blocking before attempting to grab also gives you a sense of your opponent's rhythm. This is especially important if he is wielding a knife. Don't attempt to grab his knife-wielding hand in midair and disarm him. Rather block, parry, or slap his arm away to get a feel for his rhythm and stall his momentum, and on a subsequent move, block and grab.

If you are the knife-wielding fighter, however, we recommended keeping your hands free rather than attempting to control your opponent through grabs. Since you have access to a knife, you also have the capacity to end the fight in just a few strikes. There should be no need to grab your adversary. Success requires thinking beyond the first move. Try to work your techniques into patterns of threes. One or two strikes may not be enough to hurt, overwhelm, or subdue an attacker. More than three may make you tired or sloppy, and may not give you the opportunity to note your opponent's reaction. Thinking beyond the first move will also help improve speed. This is particularly true if applying the acceleration concept, which states that each subsequent strike should be faster than the one before; in other words, the second strike should be faster than the first, but slower than the third.

Each technique must be fully pronounced in order to prove effective. When we pick up speed, we tend to become sloppy with our techniques; we fail to pronounce them. Speed is increased by shortening the moves and eliminating pauses. Try to equate the techniques to the simple concept of walking. It should take no more effort. Once you have learned each individual move well, as somebody said, you just "walk a little faster."

Instead of slashing or stabbing repeatedly, mixing a single slash and stab might prove useful, too, when learning about speed. A slash comes from an angle toward or away from the centerline, while a stab follows a linear path. Mixing these two types of strikes makes it difficult for your opponent to find a predictable rhythm, and therefore difficult to defend himself.

Now explore how to defend against a knife or empty-hand technique, using only a single strike with the knife, or launching the finishing blow with just one or two strikes instead of a full technique. How can these concepts be applied to empty-hand martial arts, where the finishing strike follows the initial block to shorten the technique and gain time?

PRESSING THE ATTACK

Pressing the attack is a concept that applies to your empty-hand martial art, and also to when you are armed with a weapon and in need to defend yourself. There must be offense, because offense alone hurts your opponent enough to take away his or her fighting spirit or force him to retreat. Another concept involves closing the distance. You need the knowledge to end the fight, whether it is done with a punch, kick, grab, or joint manipulation technique. But you cannot utilize your skill and end the fight unless you can reach your opponent. Once you have closed the distance, be like a leech, always in your opponent's face. Multiple strikes have the power to turn the fight to your advantage. Multiple strikes interfere with your opponent's defense. Multiple strikes overwhelm him or her, cause trauma, and establish your reputation as a fighter. Multiple strikes leave your opponent no breathing room. Blocks and avoidance are not purely defensive moves, but rather ways to receive your opponent's attack and control it. Pressing the attack disrupts your opponent's mental faculties and forces him or her into a defensive attitude. When you disrupt his mind, you disrupt his techniques. When you take away his ability to move as he wishes, his plans fail and he will be sorry he engaged you.

Seeking the initiative, acting before your opponent acts, being mentally prepared and aware of your surroundings gives you superiority to the point that you can catch your opponent off guard, beat him to the punch (or stab or slash), and take advantage of a window of opportunity to finish the fight. Enter the confrontation with confidence and strike with authority. Be fully prepared to defend yourself, and counterattack hard enough to establish your reputation and teach your opponent that your skills are not to be taken lightly. Confidence is gained by being in charge, by seeking the initiative, by deciding how, where, and when; in other words, by pressing the attack. This is true whether empty-handed or armed with a knife.

Much of pressing the attack involves counterstriking. Think offense. When your opponent strikes, parry or block and counter immediately. When he or she reaches out to grab you, parry or block and counter immediately. Move and counterstrike, or interfere with his moves and counterstrikes. But whatever you do, you must counterstrike. This might be particularly important if your opponent, too, is wielding a knife, or if he is the only one wielding a knife and you are empty-handed and therefore at a severe disadvantage. The last thing you want is to engage in knife dueling. Knife defense conducted properly is not a trade-off in blows. It's about seizing the initiative and ending the fight as quickly as possible, which necessarily requires offense following the first defensive move. Don't allow your opponent to regroup after the first block or strike; don't give him the chance to retake the initiative. Stay a step ahead of your adversary, always.

Ideally, your defense against the first strike places you in position to escalate the fight and build on successive techniques until you can wage that final damaging blow that ends the battle. If you can, eliminate the pause between defense and offense. The moment you block a strike is a signal to continue with a technique that ends the fight, or at least interferes enough with your opponent's movement to prevent him or her from throwing another strike. Do not block, pause, and counterstrike. Rather, block and counterstrike almost simultaneously.

Furthermore, since no single strike is guaranteed to end the fight instantly, when a strike fails to do the necessary damage, be prepared to follow with another strike to another target or to the same target. Defense without offense or defense without follow-up is useless because, although it might help you avoid the first strike, it will not help you win the fight.

Thus, when your opponent blocks or redirects your attack, an important concept is to avoid freezing or stalling your defensive technique or counterattack. This is particularly true when you have a knife in your hand, because by stalling your motion, you also present an opportunity for your opponent to disarm you. The moment your attack is blocked, it should be a signal to redirect the blade of the knife toward any area on your opponent's arm or body where skin is exposed. Remember that the knife is a touch weapon; it does not require a great deal of power to prove effective. A simple twist of your hand may be enough to cut your opponent's hand or arm. If your empty-hand martial art calls for trapping your opponent's arm the moment you block his attack, a slight variation of the move that allows the blade to contact and cut bare skin can be used when wielding a knife. If your opponent is proficient at blocking your attack, you may need to change from linear to circular motion in order to penetrate his defense and avoid getting disarmed.

DISTANCE AND POSITIONING

Just as distance and positioning are extremely important in empty-hand martial arts, because without proper distance and positioning you can't reach your opponent with a powerful strike (too far away, and you can't reach him at all; too close, and you will stifle your power), proper distance and positioning are important when armed with a knife. But, due to the inherent qualities of an edged weapon (sharpness, ease of concealment, etc.), you might need to view distance and positioning from a slightly different perspective. For instance, it might benefit you to get as close as possible to your opponent before deploying your weapon and attacking. This gives him less time to react to your attack and decreases the risk that you will telegraph your intentions. For example, if your plan is to attack with a stab to the midsection, rather than exposing the knife from a distance as you move forward, keep it by your hip or concealed in your hand. When within a foot or two of your opponent, deploy the knife and stab straight to the midsection. If your opponent hasn't perceived the threat by then, he will get cut. If you reverse the scenario and an adversary is advancing toward you, remember that he might have a knife. If you allow him to get to close range before you throw a preemptive strike, it may be too late.

When using a knife instead of your empty hand, you derive certain benefits in distance and positioning as well as in speed, which allow for adjustments in stance and movement. An overhead stab, for instance, does not need to start high above your head, where your opponent has the opportunity to block it. Start with the knife by your hip instead, or concealed behind your forearm. When within reach, draw your arm up quickly and immediately stab downward. Defending against such an attack with the typical upward block will prove difficult.

Slashes are very fast and can easily follow a tight figure-eight pattern, using circular moves to reverse directions and flow from one slash to the next. Many empty-hand martial arts likewise use circular moves to redirect or trap an adversary's strike, before reverting to a linear strike. When training with the knife instead of the bare fist, explore slashes from forward and reverse grip in a figure-eight or circular/semi-circular pattern. Upon completing a slash, reverse motion and stab linearly to a vital target.

Try these exercises for gaining a better understanding of distance and positioning (with training knives, of course):

1. With the knife in forward grip, face your partner and extend your arm straight toward him until the tip of the knife barely touches his body. To execute an effective cut from this distance, you need to take a step forward or pivot your body considerably to close the gap and achieve at least a few inches penetration.

2. Bend your arm until your elbow is in close proximity to your body. Your opponent will feel tempted to close the gap, because in his mind, he is in his zone of safety as long as the tip of the knife does not reach him. But it is a visual illusion. You can now reach him with the knife simply by extending your arm a few inches. Since the knife is a touch weapon, it can do damage also without full body rotation. You can even do considerable damage with the knife from a square (horse) stance.

Be aware that an opponent armed with the knife can defeat you quickly simply by extending his arm, even if he does not employ body rotation. Image source: Martina Sprague.

MOVEMENT AND FOOTWORK

Your empty-hand martial art has probably taught you to take ground, or as previously discussed, to press the attack, because it is more difficult for your opponent to fight effectively when forced to backpedal or when off balance. When backpedaling, he cannot use momentum to his advantage, and he also does not know what is behind him that may place him in an unfavorable position or on the ground. When off balance, as you probably know from your own training, your techniques will lose most of their power.

Movement and footwork when armed with a knife can be practiced at first with the help of a heavy bag or focus mitt held by your partner. As you experiment with stance and movement in the spirit of your martial art, consider whether you can be more successful with the knife held in your lead or rear hand. Although there is no single best answer to this question, it is recommended that the knife be held in your lead hand most of the time, because it places the knife closer to the threat and gives you the greatest reach. A drawback is that it decreases your ability to conceal the knife and places you at greater risk of getting disarmed.

As in your empty-hand martial art, assuming a superior position to the outside of your opponent (away from his centerline) is generally safer than assuming a position along his centerline, because remaining to the outside of his body restricts the use of his arms and legs. But it may also make it more difficult to reach primary targets on his torso, such as the heart or other organs housed in the body. The kidney is a target you can generally reach when positioned to the outside of your opponent. Also, don't forget targets on the legs, such as the tendons behind the knee, a slash to which could drop your opponent to the ground and render him incapable of continuing the fight.

Historical Gem: With respect to movement and footwork, Japanese swordsman Miyamoto Musashi, in his *Book of Five Rings*, advises us to reflect an inwardly calm through our martial arts stance. Your stance should neither be threatening nor timid, yet ready to meet any danger. When your combat stance is as natural as possible, you can live each day normally as if there were no dangers, yet always be ready for battle. Assuming a stance with your guard high when someone offends you may not only escalate an encounter, but give your opponent plenty of warning to ready his forces. Assuming a normal stance, by contrast, brings uncertainty to the mind of the opponent. He will not know when or how you will attack.

Just as your stance should resemble a posture as normal as possible, so should your footwork. When moving forward, back, and to the side, whether moving fast or slow, your footwork should resemble normal walking. Many martial arts teach to fight with one side of the body continuously facing forward. Boxers, for example, normally fight with their left side forward and their right side back if they are right-handed, to place their stronger side to the rear and give their strikes a longer distance for building momentum. A karate fighter often places his stronger side forward to give his lead strikes greater speed through a shorter distance to the target. The skilled samurai, by contrast, moved the way one normally walks, in an alternating right-left stride for balance and speed when cutting, warding off blows, or withdrawing after an attack. Every move with the sword was accompanied by a right-left or left-right step, which allowed him to retain control of movement and seize the initiative from the enemy. The samurai never remained in the same spot and therefore did not become an easy target for his opponent's counterattack. When he thought of footwork the way he thought of walking, he was always ready to meet and defend against an attack.

DISARMING THE OPPONENT OR NOT?

Be aware that your opponent or practice partner might feel tempted to disarm you, particularly if your empty-hand martial art involves grabs, traps, takedowns, or throws. Think about how to counter a disarming attempt. For instance, if your opponent grabs your knife hand or arm and pulls you toward him forcefully, a slight redirection of the blade may force him to abandon his disarming attempt to avoid getting cut. The moment he reacts is the time to seize the initiative. If this technique were done empty-handed; for example, if you threw a strike that your opponent intercepted and grabbed in an attempt to continue your momentum and throw you off balance, what technique would you use to counter his attempt? Explore empty-handed before picking up the knife. Now, when your opponent intercepts or blocks your knife attack, explore how to go with the motion, perhaps with a slight redirection of the blade, into a new attack. If you are thrown off balance, explore how to go with the motion to recover your balance and also use the momentum to instigate a counterattack.

When practicing knife disarming techniques, if you are not well-versed and have no idea of the different ways to wield and attack with a knife, if you don't know the strengths and weaknesses of each grip, you are cheating yourself out of what might be life saving knowledge. So, should you disarm your opponent or not? As long as your assailant's weapon is not in a position where it is a direct threat to your life or safety, you may be better off letting him or her keep it initially. At this stage of your training, you might want to examine how to limit an assailant's effectiveness by *not* disarming him. As you proceed, consider how a person who attacks with a weapon is likely to have tunnel vision and think only of attacking with the weapon. This means that he is not focused on what his other hand is doing, or how well he is maintaining his foundation. Perhaps you can limit his effectiveness with the knife by using your longer reaching legs to kick his kneecap. Or, if you are exceptionally skilled at joint controlling techniques, perhaps you can find an opportunity to control your adversary's free hand, thereby causing him so much pain that he cannot attack with the knife.

One way to "disarm" your opponent without disarming him of the knife, is by inflicting pain so severe that he can no longer focus on attacking with the weapon. Image source: Martina Sprague.

Although it is obviously a good idea to control the weapon when defending against a knife attack, when we hear the phrase "control the weapon," we tend to think of different ways in which to disarm the opponent. But it is not really the weapon that should be controlled, but rather the opponent's ability to use the weapon. This leaves us with several possibilities, each with its own pros and cons. For example:

1. You can control the use of the weapon by disarming the adversary and taking the weapon from him, and perhaps using it against him.

2. You can control the use of the weapon by disarming him and letting the weapon fall to the ground. But this comes with the risk of someone else, perhaps an accomplice, picking up the weapon and using it against you.

3. You can control the use of the weapon through positioning, so that the adversary cannot reach you with the weapon; for example, by taking his balance.

4. You can control the use of the weapon by attacking a primary target, such as his eyes, with your empty hand or fingers without even touching the weapon or weapon hand.

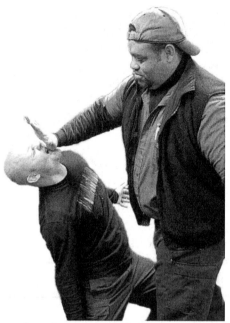

The eyes, or face in general, is a good target to strike initially. A strike to the eyes or face may distract your adversary enough to "disarm" him without gaining physical control of his weapon. Image source: Martina Sprague.

Compare these concepts to your empty-hand martial art, where your goal is likewise to control the opponent's use of his weapons. If he is off balance, he cannot strike or kick effectively. If he cannot see, he cannot use his hands or feet against you. If you manage to control him through joint manipulation, he will not be in position to use his hands or feet, because his full focus will be on the pain in his joint.

You can indirectly control all of your opponent's weapons by disturbing his balance; for example, by pushing, sweeping, throwing, or otherwise taking him down. The moment your opponent begins to lose his balance, all of his techniques will be useless, no matter how big, strong, or well-trained he is. Whether or not you actually place him on the ground may be irrelevant, as long as you upset his physical and mental harmony long enough to halt his attack and destroy his momentum. Now take advantage of your position by launching a finishing strike.

It has been said that a weapon is only as good as the person using it. A weapon can't work miracles by itself, and a risk weapon-wielders face is becoming obsessed with the weapon. When wielding a weapon, you don't *have* to end the fight through the use of that weapon. Explore how to use strikes, kicks, and grabs in conjunction with the knife. Although a weapon can help you succeed, it can also hinder performance. When blocking or grabbing your opponent's knife hand, remember that your free hand and feet are still available for use. The fight should not become a physical struggle over who gets the knife. If you are wielding the knife and your opponent grabs your knife hand, rather than struggling to free that hand, use your other hand or legs to attack the assailant.

When you have trained in a particular style of martial art, you are also likely to have trained with others in that particular style. Consider the fact that your training partners are normally cooperative. Although training with cooperative partners is necessary for good learning to take place, once you rise in the ranks, you need to include more chaos in training, making it as realistic as possible. Since every person may not be able to use every technique to the same degree of proficiency, you may not know what it really takes to unbalance an assailant, to wrestle him or her to the ground, and to disarm him of an edged weapon.

FURTHERING THE LEARNING EXPERIENCE

Martial arts are not a mindless rut. With understanding comes mastery. Don't be satisfied with simply naming the technique, weapon, or target. Also explain why you would attack a specific target in a specific way. To really demonstrate understanding of martial arts practice with the knife, attempt to explain the details of a technique to other students in your class. Or, if practicing alone at home, explain the details and concepts that go along with a technique to yourself. For example, talk about a situation that might require defense using a knife, and how you would use the knife to stop your opponent's initial strike, regardless of whether he is also armed with a knife or is empty-handed. Name the particular strike and target that would likely end the fight and explain why. For example, a block to your opponent's forearm or wrist would not necessarily end the fight; although, it would allow you to defend against his initial attack. When you follow with a slash across his neck, however, this would end the fight, because the blood vessels in the neck are near the surface of the skin and can easily be cut even if there is only slight penetration with the knife. When these blood vessels are cut, the brain will no longer be supplied with the blood it needs to function, so the fight will end.

Purposeful practice stimulates insightful learning, gives the techniques meaning, and eliminates simple imitation of performance. When you have gained a basic understanding of the knife techniques you are studying, explaining to others how and why a technique is done is a good learning tool, because it forces you to think. If you are unable to answer a question that is posed, you must find the answer through independent study or by asking someone else. When you can explain techniques correctly, you have demonstrated evidence of understanding. When you reach the intermediate and advanced levels, you may be able to explain the concepts of a technique in which you have not yet received instruction, simply because the technique is similar to another technique that you have already learned. Theoretical understanding alone may not enable you to perform the technique, however. Proficiency in performance comes with practice over a period of time. But proficient performance without understanding is mechanical and useless in situations that require adaptation to the surrounding circumstances. Understanding and performing therefore go hand-in-hand and should be nurtured together.

Generally, you can perform a technique with reasonable proficiency before you develop insight. You can test your understanding and ability to apply the technique by demonstrating your skills under less predictable circumstances, and by asking the "W-questions":

1. What is the purpose of the technique?

2. When would I use it?

3. Who would I use it against?

4. How are the moves put together?

5. Why this way?

6. What if . . .?

When you have gained basic understanding and ability to apply the technique, the next stage is to learn how the material relates to other material that you have not yet learned. You can now use what you have learned from one technique and apply it to another. Or you can apply what you have learned in your empty-hand martial art to knife fighting, and vice versa. You can teach yourself new techniques and concepts and answer questions about techniques that you have never practiced or experienced. You will begin to see similarities between different martial arts and will come to appreciate other arts more. You can now explore how one technique or concept is similar to or relates to another technique or concept. For example:

1. When learning the horizontal elbow strike, start by reviewing the hook since both strikes follow the same *striking pattern*.

2. After learning the horizontal elbow strike, learn the downward elbow strike by relating it to the horizontal elbow strike since both strikes utilize the same *striking weapon*.

3. After learning these empty-hand techniques, pick up a knife and learn how the motion of these empty-hand techniques can be used also when wielding a knife in the forward or reverse grip.

A hook follows essentially the same striking pattern

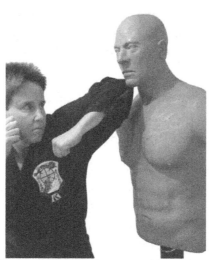

as an elbow strike. When would you use either technique? When would you use a knife in the motion of a hook or elbow strike? Image source: Martina Sprague.

Knowledge and education require critical thinking skills. Education comes through a combination of theoretical study and practical application. Don't merely take another person for his or her words. For instance, if your instructor or another student mentions that the so-called "blood groove" (the fullered part of the blade) has as its purpose to relieve suction when the knife is stabbed into the target by allowing blood to flow along this groove, don't take his or her word for it. Go home and research the purpose of a fullered blade. You might be surprised at what you find. When you have done your research, you will not continue to perpetuate a myth to your own students.

Thus, although book learning should complement your martial arts training, physical practice and analysis is still essential. As in your empty-hand martial art, when armed with a knife, you must choose to fight a decisive battle; you must be physically and mentally prepared to use your weapon to end the fight. Whatever stance you use, it should communicate combat readiness; you should aim all blocks and strikes at realistic targets. Strip away the shrouds of mystery that sometimes surround the martial arts, and examine the situation with a clear eye. Although you have learned specific martial arts techniques, you must study the concepts behind them and learn to apply them also when armed with a knife. Discuss with others the meaning of decisive victory.

Your skill also increases when you practice your art consistently and with intent, when you make realistic self-evaluations, and when you have an inquisitive mind and have thought about your goals and the requirements to attain them. Understand that no one size fits all and that learning must be tailored to your particular needs. Continuously seek to improve yourself by keeping an open mind, yet striving to stay with the times and modifying outdated techniques and thinking patterns.

As you move forward, remember, too, that martial artists are deeply opinionated, and often rightly so. There is seldom if ever only one way of doing a technique, and the precise method we choose often depends on our particular background, the type of martial art we have studied, and our personal experiences. A law enforcement officer will look at the dangers of the knife from a different perspective than a martial artist in the training hall. A soldier in a combat zone will view the knife differently than a street gang member. The *Knife Training Methods and Techniques for Martial Artists* series has hopefully demonstrated that there are many ways to think about and practice martial arts and knife fighting. However, the "best" way will probably continue to be debated forever.

Historical Gem: Consider this statement by Miyamoto Musashi, perhaps the greatest Japanese swordsman of all time: "The views of each school, and the logic of each path, are realized differently according to the individual person." See Miyamoto Musashi, *The Book of Five Rings*, translated by Thomas Cleary (Boston, MA: Shambala, 2000), 58.

SOMETHING TO THINK ABOUT FOR FUTURE TRAINING

As Western martial artists, we view and train with the knife in a way that suits our Western mindset. This makes us predictable to a degree. Although it is very difficult to defend against a knife-wielding assailant, particularly if we are taken by surprise, we still have some idea of how the attack is likely to happen and the type of knife we are likely to encounter. It will probably be either a stab or slash, and it will probably be done with the knife either in forward or reverse grip. And the knife will probably be a straight blade, either single- or double-edge. It might have a bit of a clip tip, or it might be a folder type knife. Although there are several possible variations within these knife designs, we probably will not expect to encounter a machete, or a *kukri*, or an Indonesian *kris*. We will probably not expect a quick upward slash from groin to sternum with a curved and easily concealable *karambit*, as pictured in Book 1 of the *Knife Training Methods and Techniques for Martial Artists* series. This is why we must stress the importance of training in knife offense with a variety of knife types and designs, because it is utterly difficult to understand how to defend against such attacks, if we don't first understand how different blades are meant to be used.

Although we possibly might, we probably won't encounter an attack with a *karambit* that eviscerates us from groin to sternum. Image source: Martina Sprague.

That said, if you frequent non-Western countries with different customs and different ways of fighting empty-hand or with a weapon, to be effective in a real self-defense situation, you must know something about the weapons and the culture. As Western martial artists, although we enjoy studying ancient Asian martial arts, we are bound by our own time, culture, and circumstance. We might be fascinated by the Japanese samurai, but most of us would not carry nor encounter a *katana* in a street fight. We might admire the Nepalese Gurkhas, but will probably not carry nor encounter a *kukri*. When we debate the "best" fighting knife, or the "best" way to use a knife in offense or defense against an attack, we must also consider the type of blade that is likely to be carried in our particular part of the world.

With the previous in mind, and what I really hope you will take away from the *Knife Training Methods and Techniques for Martial Artists* series of books, as the name states, is that the series is really about knife training for martial artists. It is not about knife training for soldiers in a war zone, nor for law enforcement personnel, nor for street thugs. Moreover, as a martial artist, you don't have to train with the knife only, or even at all, for the purpose of self-defense. There are many reasons other than self-defense why a martial artist chooses to learn about knife offense and defense. For example, you might be training with bladed weapons in order to improve your timing and enhance your empty-hand techniques; you might be training because you have an interest in the historical aspects of the knife, in which case it would make sense to train with exotic blades that are not part of our Western culture; or you might be training with knives simply because you think it is fun. During your continued training, you may well discover new insights into knife offense and defense that are not mentioned in this series of books, and that will help you grow both as a person and martial artist.

About the author:

Martina Sprague is a military historian and martial artist. She has studied the martial arts since 1987 and holds black belts in Kenpo karate, kickboxing, and street freestyle. She is the author of numerous martial arts and military history books. For more information, please visit her Web site: www.modernfighter.com.

Made in the USA
Las Vegas, NV
01 February 2021